ONÓRIO CUTANE

The Spiritual World

Understanding How Spiritual Forces Dictate the Life of Humans on Earth

ARPress

ARPress
45 Dan Road Suite 5
Canton MA 02021
Hotline: 1(888) 821-0229
Fax: 1(508) 545-7580

Ordering Information:
Quantity sales. Special discounts are available on quantity purchases by corporations, associations, and others. For details, contact the publisher at the address above.

Printed in the United States of America.

ISBN-13:   Softcover   979-8-89389-515-5
             eBook   979-8-89389-516-2

Library of Congress Control Number: 2024919517

TABLE OF CONTENTS

PREFACE

This piece is an epiphany to understanding the supernatural factors that influence the lives of humans on eartth. It's a treaty on the spiritual world and the spiritual actors composing it in its various organizations and hierarchical structures.

This book's general objective is to open the curtains, remove the scales from human eyes, and give a detailed understanding of the spiritual forces that dictate the lives of men here on earth. But, first, you must understand that there is a dimension above the physical one. It is the fourth dimension, or also called the spiritual dimension. In it, angelic actors, belonging to two antagonistic realms, interact with their agendas - some for and some against the life of human beings on earth.

Furthermore, it aims to awaken our understanding that not everything we see with our physical eyes is all that exists in our world. We live alongside beings from other dimensions and layers - the angelic beings of good and/or evil.

In the Saint John book, verse 1:51 (NIV), Jesus states, "He then added, "Very truly I tell you, you will see 'heaven open, and the angels of God ascending and descending on'the Son of Man." Thus, Jesus reveals to us his daily experience as God's angels ministered to Him.

The physical contemporaries of Jesus and even most of his followers didn't have the same experience because their eyes were still closed to the reality of the spiritual world. Furthermore, we have Stephen's example, who, due to the pressure from his detractors, experienced a glory of such dimension that it was seen as madness by them. In practice, he was the only person among them all to see what they didn't see, "the spiritual world." Here are his words, "Look, I see heaven open and the Son of Man standing at the right hand of God." In that dimension, he spoke to the Lord Jesus as one who saw him physically as well as the glory of God and said, "Lord Jesus, receive my spirit" (Acts 7:56-59 NIV). What a glorious experience Stephen had! Something above this world. How was it that he had access to this spiritual dimension hidden from the rest of humans? The scripture makes it clear, "But Stephen, full of the Holy Spirit, looked up to heaven and saw the glory of God, and Jesus standing at the right hand of God" (Acts 7:55

NIV). It was through the Holy Spirit. He was filled with the Spirit. The Holy Spirit helps us experience the fourth dimension so that we live in Him, walk in Him, and operate from Him consciously. Unfortunately, many of God's children have not yet taken advantage of the glories of this dimension. Some for lack of knowledge and others for lack of a practical, experiential experience with the Holy Spirit.

It reminds me of the peace, tranquility, and security Elisha experienced in his life. While his servant was fearful, apprehensive, and frozen with the apparent circumstances he saw, the two of them were in the same physical place, had heads, arms, and legs, and wore clothes. They were eating and drinking water. Apparently, from a human point of view, they were similar, save for a few traits that distinguished each person. Moreover, they faced the same challenge: the Assyrian soldiers who surrounded them intending to capture them at the behest of the wicked king. Physically, they were in a flat place and their detractors on a hill. But, in the human eye, they were at a dead-end, a labyrinth. This was how Elisha's young helper saw things. They had the same God but not the same experiences.

Fearful and frozen, the young man says, "My lord, what shall I do." He thinks about acting humanely. Run away? There is no way. Surrender? It seems obvious. But what does the prophet, the man of God, say? Why is he not afraid or apprehensive? What does he trust? What does he see that others don't, and what does he know about this God that others don't? How can he have such a calm and positive reaction to life? There could be several questions listed here, but the answer brings us to one point: although they were physically in the same place, spiritually, they were in opposite positions, in different dimensions in terms of advantage. The young man was carnal, characteristic of ordinary human beings, who have not yet experienced a spiritual dimension above the human one. Elisha prayed for him. What did he ask for? That God would open his eyes to see what was there and experience the glories of the higher dimension. That is what this book seeks to do: reveal and open your eyes to understand the world beyond our physical one, the world that surrounds us - the spiritual world.

Your life depends on what happens in the spiritual world or spiritual arena. Your victories, progress, and evolution depend on the consciousness, knowledge, and understanding you have of this arena.

This world pre-exists every human being, but we don't give it its due importance out of ignorance. And consequently, it is partially presented to us in difficult circumstances: diseases, illnesses of various kinds, inexplicable separations, deaths, breaks in the rhythm of life, among others. Thus, the guidance given is part of this somewhat imaginary world, not natural and from which a human being can provide the means to get around it.

The young man, Elisha's servant, had the grace to walk with a man of God who not only knew this spiritual world but also had experienced and lived in it consciously. In this arena, Elisha spoke words, and something happened. He would decree something that materialized. He lived connected to a powerful world, and his life was continually miraculous and naturally inexplicable. It was a supernatural life.

Dear reader, you too can experience the glory that God manifested, which is present in this dimension. It is your portion as a child of God. This is why God wants to fill all humanity with the Holy Spirit so that they will no longer be carnal but spiritual, living the life He destined for them: a life of glory and victory that Adam lost because of the sin that led him to his fall. Your body is an imitation of the divinity; there is more to the earth than you can see and hear.

Elisha's young servant wasn't only young in age, that wasn't a problem because even Jeremiah was called young, and John of Revelation was the youngest apostle among the others. David was a teenager when he killed Goliath, but he was also young in spiritual experiences, in the knowledge of this dimension that surrounded him daily. Imagine, he would have passed from this world without ever having experienced what was available to him. So, the Holy Spirit imprinted in my heart that I write this book for the children of God to receive the grace to live and operate from this dimension. It is all around you now, at this very moment, influencing every aspect of your life and your community, family, and alike.

Subdivisions of the spiritual world

Understand that the spirit world consists of two subdivisions: the one operated by God's angels for the benefit of God's people, and the other operated by the fallen angels and demons, trying to destroy, steal and kill on earth. Unfortunately, the devil's servants or agents, that is, the wizards and witches, have been very successful in their diabolical operations and incursions. That's because they are aware of their dimension, have been initiated into it, and have received their powers and gallons of blood, which they drink per day, from the devil, to whom they give reports. The forces of evil have always hated man, the upright, righteous, and God-fearing man. This is because the devil is man's number one enemy. He operates from this dimension, trying to destroy man's life. How does a wizard, from a mirror, manage to make someone's face appear and cast a plague on him that may result in death or destruction of the person's life or cause him madness and other kinds of evils? It's our duty as children of the light to stop such incursions.

This book contributes to Christian literature, seeking to provide, equip and supply believers with knowledge of the spirit world, its dimensions, and the consequences of choosing the spirit world - an arena of evil or good. By understanding and applying the knowledge from this book, I hope the reader will live above this world's circumstances and the evil attacks of man's enemy: the devil.

Dear reader, understand that we have greater power than all the wizards and witches put together. We have control over all spiritual hosts of wickedness. However, it takes revelational knowledge to walk with dominion in this sphere. Even God said, "My people are destroyed from lack of knowledge" (Hosea 4:6 NIV). The destruction didn't come because the devil is strong, or the executioner forces are more powerful, but because of the lack of divine and revelational knowledge. This book seeks to provide some of this knowledge as a contribution to Christian literature.

Elisha prays for his servant to see

"And Elisha prayed, "Open his eyes, LORD, so that he may see." We notice here that there was prayer involved for Elisha's servant to access this dimension. Elisha prayed for him. And, what happened next? The Scripture continues, "Then the LORD opened the servant's eyes, and he looked and saw the hills full of horses and chariots of fire all around Elisha" (2 Kings 6:17 NIV). Before that, Elisha had said to the young man, "Don't be afraid, those who are with us are more than those who are with them" (Verse 16). Who were they? God's angels, the horses, and chariots of war surrounding the prophet, protecting him and the nation of Israel. Even the young man was benefiting from this protection without knowing it. Through Elisha's prayer, his servant changes dimensions in the blink of an eye: he transcends from the human dimension, where fear and terror tormented his heart, to the spiritual, where faith and the presence of God's angels produce peace, joy, and victory. In the blink of an eye, the young man's fear disappears, and he discovers that all the time he has been fearful and downcast, he should have been quiet and enjoying the presence and glory of God. But this is how the life of many believers in the whole world has been; they don't know who they are, what they have, and where they are in Christ. Due to this, they live defeated lives, occasionally experiencing the glory of God in minute doses, instead of enjoying the fullness and abundance at their disposal.

Elisha went further, with prayer, and got God to put blindness in the eyes of those invading soldiers. Even with their human eyes seemingly open, confusion came to their minds. They were confused and guided by Elisha's word to the center of the city of Samaria as defeated. Elisha prays for them, and their blindness is removed, and they realize that they are the ones now in ambush. The ambush they had set against God's people served them instead, as if for them to taste a dose of their own medicine.

Vision Gradation

Opening the open eyes and closing the already closed eyes

Dear reader, notice this: Elisha's young servant had his human eyes open and didn't see the spiritual reality. When Elisha prayed for him, the eyes that were apparently open opened again. How? How can you open eyes that are already open? Simple! This reveals that the power of God came upon the young man's natural eyes, enabling them to see more than they saw before. The Spirit of God increased his eyes' gradation. Soon, he began to experience a dimension greater than human, greater than what he was subject to before; he experienced the fourth dimension, the spiritual world of the department operated by God's who were walking with Elisha and the nation of Israel.

The Assyrian soldiers, on the other hand, came with their eyes open, and when Elisha prayed to the Lord to smite them with blindness, the eyes they had seen with continued to see what they shouldn't have been seeing. It's not that they became humanly blind and started groping around looking for someone to guide them! No. They thought they saw, when in fact, they couldn't see the reality that surrounded them.

Oh my God! How many people are at this stage in life! They think they see, when in fact, they don't see further than the capacity of their eyes to see. They are so deceived that they make wrong choices, live immoral lives, and end up knowingly going into the grave. Sometimes, you see people who work from January to November but don't see what they do with their money. They are living as if their minds are alienated from them, like sheep to the slaughterhouse. They don't wake up; they don't see or react. They are entirely tamed by spiritual blindness. They count the years of their lives, but their years don't seem to matter. Stalled in time and space: bound by the princes of darkness and the spiritual hosts of wickedness in the heavenly places. They are bound but still walking and running - inside a cage. It is freedom in the form of a mirage. They sow, and the devil comes to reap, they gather, and the devil comes to scatter, but they don't know or understand; they continue to walk in darkness. They are resigned to mediocrity, poverty, barrenness, stagnation, and others even commit suicide, ending their own lives without first completing the curses that continue to extend to their children and grandchildren like streams of water. Why? Because they don't understand that life is spiritual and there are extraterrestrial forces, spiritual forces that dictate the course of human life on earth.

This book was written to help the people of God in particular, and humanity in general, get rid of all the negative influences of the kingdom of darkness and enforce the Kingdom of Heaven on earth: the kingdom of Jesus Christ, Lord of lords and King of kings.

This book will give you tools to successfully fight spiritual battles because we are at war, a war against the devil and his spiritual and physical agents.

Jesus won on the cross: Heaven and hell know it, but humans on earth still need to understand this eternal truth: light always prevails over darkness, and good always overcomes evil, no matter how long it seems to take or how much impunity injustice seems to enjoy.

For this, you have to do something here on earth from the spiritual arena; God will not do everything without man's intervention. The Scripture says, "The highest heavens belong to the LORD, but the earth he has given to mankind" (Psalm 115:16 NIV).

Dear reader, this is our land, which God gave Adam to man, not the devil. He usurped it from the first Adam, but Jesus - the second Adam, got it back for us. Therefore, we will not tolerate the devil's influence in our times. We will paralyze his activities in all aspects of the sphere of human life. It's our sovereign responsibility.

This is our time; this is our moment: the era of the glory of God's children. The earth groans and waits for the manifestation of the children of God.

Structure of the book

The book is organized into 33 chapters. It presents an easy-to-understand language with explanations and concrete examples of the correlation between the spiritual and the physical, divine and the human. Throughout the book, we use the terms: Word of God, Holy Scripture, and Holy Bible interchangeably, i.e., one in place of the other, with the same meaning.

Read it calmly and with an open heart, absorbing the revelations it contains and digesting them in meditation. Then, put into practice the knowledge and guidance that God's Spirit presents to you. Finally, see yourself living in victory and for the glory of the Lord Jesus, extending His kingdom on earth until He returns.

God bless you richly

INTRODUCTION

Understanding the concept of the spiritual world

"Praise be to the God and Father of our Lord Jesus Christ, who has blessed us in the heavenly realms with every spiritual blessing in Christ" (Ephesians 1:3 NIV).

In his description, St. Paul defines the God to whom we worship - God and the father of our Lord Jesus Christ; an accuracy that excludes all possible divinities and all eventual idols that people worshipped. This God created the earth and Heaven, life, man and the universe, and everything in it. This God is Jehovah - the self-existing and eternal God, father of our savior Jesus Christ. The apostle Paul described this God because he was aware that there were many gods that men worshiped.

Dear reader, from today on, you must look at life from the spiritual plane, the spiritual vision, that is, from the spiritual arena or the spiritual world, hallelujah.

Conceptualization

The spirit world is a sphere of spiritual activities. It is a superhuman dimension where spiritual beings and agents who have no natural physical body operate. There are several synonyms with the same semantic charge, or there are plurivalent. For example, we can call it the spiritual world, spiritual arena, spiritual sphere, or the spiritual atmosphere, and we are still talking about the same polysemic concept. These are called heavenly places.

The spirit world is much more accurate than the physical world we live in; believe this and let no one deceive you or tell you otherwise. Furthermore, the spiritual world was the first to be created by God before the physical world existed.

Everything on earth, everything that is matter, generally presents three dimensions or three planes that can be seen and observed. However, there is another (extra) plane that isn't scientifically observable, and it's called "The Fourth Dimension," which is the spiritual or immaterial dimension. And it's this fourth dimension that we are dealing with in this book. What happens in the spiritual dimension directly or indirectly influences the life of human beings and physical phenomena on earth. So, therefore, we must study and understand it because it controls the three- dimensional world.

Now, we (humans) are in the three-dimensional world because we have a physical body. We have height, mass (volume), and weight, but because we are spirits, we also belong to the world of the fourth dimension. Animals cannot operate in the fourth dimension because they have no soul. When an animal dies, it's done for, but when a man dies, it's not. He leaves the physical body and transcends into both glorious eternity and torment. The body stays there, and it's often said, "So-and-so is no longer with us," but his body is there. Where did the person, that is, his spirit, go? So, we see that man's spirit continues to exist even after physical death. This suggests, therefore, that there is another world that controls this material world we are in.

The lack of knowledge and perception of this spiritual world leads to many people having their lives complicated day and night. For example, troubled marriages, barred jobs, stagnant businesses. Why? Because people cannot understand, master, manipulate, live, and walk in the four-dimensional world, which is the spiritual world.

Man, because he was created in the image and likeness of God, is a spirit and consequently belongs to the spiritual world of the fourth dimension. Still, because of the physical body, he is also in the three-dimensional world. The physical body makes the spirit legal here on earth. Those who live in the three-dimensional world always suffer drastic consequences inflicted by the spiritual agents of evil in the fourth-dimensional world. Unfortunately, there is no scientific machine that can unravel and manipulate the spiritual agents in the heavenly places, or that will make you understand what I'm going to explain to you in this book because they are spiritual matters. The Holy Bible states that the natural man doesn't understand the things of the spirit because they are spiritually discerned. You must be born again by the regeneration of the Holy Spirit and have the eyes of your understanding enlightened to understand and navigate in the spiritual world. Therefore, this new birth by faith in Jesus gives you access to receive the Holy Spirit. By being born again, we immediately find ourselves in the spiritual.

CHAPTER I

Two Essentially Distinct Worlds

Paul said, "Blessed be the God and Father of our Lord Jesus Christ, who has blessed us…." See that you can be blessed but not see or experience that blessing on the physical plane. For example, some people should already be married from the spiritual world's perspective, but in the physical world, they are still single. In the spiritual world, they should already have a house, a car, a husband or wife, and children, but there is a problem. Certain things are preventing what you have there from materializing here in the three- dimensional world. "Is that even possible, apostle?" - You may ask.

Well, I will prove it to you with concrete examples from the Holy Bible. The text in Genesis 1:26-27 (NIV) says, "Then God said, "Let us make mankind in our image, in our likeness…so God created mankind in his own image, in the image of God he created them; male and female he created them."

We notice here in this text that when God created man, he made him male and female. In other words, Adam wasn't created single; he was already married. But in Genesis 2:7, we read that God formed man from the dust of the ground. Looking at these two scriptures closely, we can notice two moments:

First: God created men;

Second: God formed men from the dust of the earth.

The creation and formation of man are not the same thing and didn't happen simultaneously. To understand this, we need to distinguish between two terms or verbs employed in these two contexts: "Create" versus "Make." Descriptively, "Create" means "to call something out of nothing," "to produce something out of nothing by calling it into existence," while "Make" means "to make something out of what already exists." Thus, it has the same meaning as a product made or processed from existing raw material.

Therefore, in the text of Genesis 2:7, we read that God formed man - Adam, only he formed him unmarried. Thus, from the dust of the earth, God formed man uniquely male. But how to explain that in chapter 1, God created him "Male and Female"? Well, this is very easy to understand. In chapter 1, we are given the notion of "marriage" or "parity," the male and female parts, respectively. Thus, Adam was already married on the spiritual plane before he was single on the physical plane.

Dear reader, understand one thing: the spirit of man has no gender; it's the physical body that presents itself configured or with feminine or masculine characteristics and traits. This is why Jesus said, "At the resurrection, people will neither marry nor be given in marriage; they will be like the angels in heaven" (Matthew 22:30 NIV). He was answering the question about a woman who had married seven brothers from the same family. By traditional law, when the husband died, his brother was to marry the woman to raise offspring for her. Now, they all died without having left offspring, and the question was about the woman's owner, "Whose wife will she be in the resurrection, since she had married the seven?" They didn't understand the things of the spirit or the spirit world.

Understand that there are heavenly bodies and earthly bodies; for each species that God creates, He also provides a body for its accommodation and functionality. The spirit is created first, and the body is formed soon after as a house to accommodate the spirit and make it lawful here on earth because a soul without a physical body has no lawfulness on earth. Remember Christ's words, "Sacrifice and offering you did not desire—but my ears you have opened—burnt offerings and sin offerings you did not require. Then I said, "Here I am, I have come—it is written about me in the scroll" (Psalm 40:6- 7 NIV). Here it speaks of a divine scroll or script where everything that the Messiah was to come to be and do was written, with details about the type of his birth, place where he would be born, the life he would lead, his ministry, his death, and resurrection. This was all planned in the spiritual world and heart of God when Christ was still the "Word" and had not become incarnate.

However, in order to fulfill all that was written about Him, He needed to have a physical body, thus leaving the spiritual world in divine migration, to the human world, to resemble men in nature. This is why He was often said to be the "Son of Man" in allusion to His human nature but at the same time retaining His divinity – being the Son of God by this same divinity. Hence, His birth didn't involve the sexual intercourse of male and female to be called "the seed of the woman."

The background here is that Christ already existed before the foundation of the world, but in spiritual form and on the spiritual plane, and the salvation of fallen humanity required that he become incarnate, "put on flesh." Why? Because He wasn't made up of flesh but by the Spirit. It's even easier to understand what I'm explaining by looking at the Scripture in Hebrews 10, verse 5 (NIV), "Therefore, when Christ came into the world, He said: Sacrifice and offering you did not desire, but a body you prepared for me." Notice something here? What was prepared for him for his functioning on earth and fulfilling his ministry or atoning work? The answer is clear: "a body." What was that body called? - Jesus. Whom did that body accommodate? - "Christ the Redeemer." Here, we see the correlation between the plans made in the timeless spiritual world and their materialization in the temporal physical world. The spiritual world is authentic, and everything good that happens on earth is planned there, announced in words, and materialized by the Holy Spirit. Likewise, the devil and his evil spiritual agents planned the bulk of the evil seen on earth and executed on earth, often by men or natural circumstances. What happens in the spiritual world moves events and circumstances in the physical world to accommodate their corresponding physical manifestation.

Creation versus formation

Back to understanding the concepts of "Creation" and "Formation" around Adam. He was created in spirit from God's Spirit, as a spiritual substance- male and female, or instead physically formed from the dust of the earth, like humus or man from clay, from the earth. He was male and female on the spiritual realm, and on the physical, he was only "male" in terms of species and sexual orientation. That's why in the text of Genesis 2:18 (NIV), God said, "It is not good for the man to be alone; I will make a helper suitable for him." And then God made Adam sleep, "Then the Lord God made a woman from the rib he had taken out of the man, and he brought her to the man" (Genesis 2:22 NIV).

God brought Eve to Adam after Adam awoke from sleep. Note that when Adam saw Eve, he didn't have to ask God who she (this creature) was - remember that until then, Adam was the only human being existing on earth. So, seeing someone with long hair, feminine features (breasts, hips, a different body with curves, with a different voice), the Holy Bible records the words that Adam said, "This is now bone of my bones and flesh of my flesh; she shall be called Woman, for she was taken out of Man" (Genesis 2:23 NIV). This shows that by revelation, he knew who she was. Notice that when Eve was created, God made Adam fall asleep, and while he was sleeping, the LORD took out one of his ribs and formed Eve - the woman. Where did Adam see her before to know who she was if, when God created her, he was in a deep sleep? It was a marriage on the physical plane (meeting and union for the first time between the two). Still, on the spiritual plane, it was some kind of reunion or matrimonial link, as if to say, "Somewhere we met, and from somewhere I know her, and I have this information within my spirit."

It's easy to understand this, keeping in mind that, according to Genesis 1:27, "male and female created them." This is why the Scripture says that the man shall leave his father and mother and be joined (cleave) to his wife, and they shall both be one flesh. Why are they both one flesh? Because in the spirit, they are one. Male and female: one in the spirit, but male and female distinct to the optical eye - in the physical. "How is that possible?" - You might question. It's God's mathematics done from the spiritual arena: two in the flesh separately, but one in the spirit unified.

CHAPTER II

Jacob versus Israel: Two dimensions of the same person

The text of Isaiah 43:1 says, "But now, this is what the Lord says—he who created you, Jacob, he who formed you, Israel: "Do not fear, for I have redeemed you; I have summoned you by name; you are mine."

Looking closely at this Holy Scripture, a question may arise, "where was Jacob before he was created?" The answer is he didn't physically exist, only in God's mind. That is why he was (had to be) created. Remember that the term "create" means to bring into existence something that didn't exist before, while "form" or "make" means to produce something from the already existing material. I already explained this in the previous chapter, but I'm repeating it for the sake of clarification.

Dear reader, have you ever heard someone say, "I create food at home; the food is ready, I have already created the dinner?" It's illogical to make this statement because, under normal conditions, one does not create dinner. Still, one makes it because the ingredients already exist, and one cooks from them because they are already available. The name "Jacob" means deceiver or supplanter. There was a time when Jacob was deceitful and, his life as Jacob was a complicated life full of adversity and trouble, for he had to live on the run from his brother Esau before the harmonious reunion.

First: Circumstances of his birth

Esau was born first, but Jacob had to cling to his brother's heel in a struggle to get out.

Second: Throughout his growth

Jacob sold a lentil stew to his older brother on the condition of exchanging the right of primogeniture: a kind of blessing and perks of inheritance and privilege given to the eldest son. Then, he tricked his father into stealing Esau's blessing, which the father pronounced on him with the mother's help in place of his older brother. Finally, his mother killed two goats and covered his hands with their skin to make him look like Esau. After Esau discovered the plot, he wanted to kill him, but Jacob fled to the land of Laban, where his uncle lives. On the way, he slept on a rock in the course of the journey. Up to this point, he had no wife, no children, no farm, and no livestock.

Arriving at Laban, his uncle's land, Jacob had to work in his house for seven years to have Rachel as his wife, but, to his "obvious" disappointment, he was given Leia, the eldest, according to practice. However, in love and with a sacrificial spirit at work, he worked another seven years to have Rachel. This whole marriage process took him fourteen years in total to marry the woman he wanted so badly. This process took a long time as if there was a spirit of tardiness and delay, trying to bar his progress, but he overcame it because of the Abrahamic blessing that his father had pronounced over him. In this (physical) dimension, Jacob's life was full of complications.

Jacob's name change by the angel of the Lord

Once, after many years of toil and deception, Jacob had an encounter with the Angel of the Lord that literally changed his life and his offspring forever. This is how the Scripture recounts it, "So Jacob was left alone, and a man wrestled with him till daybreak. When the man saw that he could not overpower him, he touched the socket of Jacob's hip so that his hip was wrenched as he wrestled with the man. Then the man said, "Let me go, for it is daybreak." But Jacob replied, "I will not let you go unless you bless me." The man asked him, "What is your name?" "Jacob," he answered. Then the man said, "Your name will no longer be Jacob, but Israel because you have struggled with God and with humans and have overcome" (Genesis 32:24-28 NIV).

From this encounter with the Angel of the Lord, Jacob's story, his name, life, family, and children changed positively. He was promoted in the spirit. That is why, to this day, we have the nation of Israel, which came about through a man's name change who had a divine and angelic encounter. As Jacob, he had a difficult life, but as Israel, he had a glorious life.

Dear reader, you must understand that promotion and elevation in life always begin in the spirit, and the fall and destruction of an individual's or a family's life also begin in the spirit. It is there where you must conquer, secure, guarantee, and protect your life, your family, business, and all aspects inherent to your life because it's from this arena where destinies are influenced, whether for good or evil, honor or dishonor, victory or defeat. Jacob's life experienced a divine promotion that left positive and indelible marks to this day. That was the angel that carried God's presence - the Angel of His presence. The word "angel" comes from the Hebrew *"Malachi"* and means "messenger." This was the messenger carrying the words, blessings, and presence of God. The Angel changed Jacob's name to Israel - a man who sees God, the one who fights with God. He became the father of a nation.

Analyzing this narrative, we can conclusively deduce that God created Jacob and then formed Israel from him, so Israel is Jacob's product. Jacob was created because he didn't exist before, but Israel was made because he lived in Jacob. Some people in the spirit already have what they are looking for. What remains now is for those things to be formed in the physical so that they will be and have what has already been freely given to them by God in the spirit. To do this, they need the help of the Holy Spirit. The Holy Bible attests, "What we have received is not the spirit of the world, but the Spirit who is from God, so that we may understand what God has freely given us" (1 Corinthians 2:12 NIV). You must be a spiritual man or woman to understand the things of the spirit, see them, and receive them freely.

CHAPTER III

You can transcend limitations and physical barriers

In another part of the Holy Bible, God said to Jeremiah, "Before I formed you in the womb I knew you before you were born I set you apart; I appointed you as a prophet to the nations" (Jeremiah 1:5 NIV). Where did God meet him? In the spirit world. When? Before he was formed in his mother's womb. Notice that he wasn't created in his mother's womb, for he already existed in the divine heart and plan. It was only his physical body that was formed in the womb to accommodate Jeremiah's spirit. In this Scripture, Jeremiah is given the outline and purpose of his life on earth as a prophet to the nations. We can look at him in two dimensions:

First: Spiritual dimension

In this, he is a great man of God and endowed with greater authority to overthrow, destroy, ruin what is evil in God's sight, and plant and build what is good and consistent with God's will. The LORD promises to be with him, urging him to always trust in his delivering and protecting power.

Second: Physical dimension

Jeremiah, still being very young and inexperienced in the visions and spiritual activities of the spiritual arena, was at first afraid of peoples' angry faces, to whom God had sent him to minister. He is young and harmless on this physical plane and placed as a sheep among wolves, which he saw as a thorny mission. Therefore, God opens his eyes to see the spiritual world through His Word, and he is trained to be the man God intended him to be: a prophet to the nations. Note God's words to Jeremiah, "What do you see, Jeremiah?" "I see the branch of an almond tree," I replied. The Lord said to me, "You have seen correctly, for I am watching[a] to see that my word is fulfilled." Here God does three things: he reminds Jeremiah of his purpose on earth, trains him in spiritual activities so that he will see and hear in the spirit, and finally assures him of the infallibility of his Word. God's Word is our spiritual navigator. That is why David considered it "your world is a lamp for my feet, a light on my path" (Psalm 119:105 NIV). All the training given to Jeremiah was through the Word of the Lord and the Holy Spirit. That is why we constantly read, "the word of the Lord came to me, saying, ..." (Jeremiah 1:4,11,12; 2:1 NIV).

To access and navigate the chain of the spirit world, you need the Holy Spirit and to spend time with God's Word. Many want to hear God's voice but don't want to study His Word. To hear God's Word clearly, you need to be on the same plane from which God speaks: the Spirit. God is Spirit, His words are spirit, and He speaks to man's spirit. You must train your spirit to walk in the spiritual world; otherwise, people may say you are crazy, or you can become a victim of the devil and his hosts of wickedness. This is why there are people who die without being what God intended them to be because they don't understand the spirit world I'm talking about. You must look at things and life from the spiritual perspective; otherwise, you may have many unanswered questions.

Speaking of Jesus, the Bible says that He is the Lamb who was slain before the foundation of the world. It doesn't say here that he was killed two thousand years ago, but that he was slain before the foundation of the world. It is a fact that, physically or historically, He was crucified, died, and resurrected from the dead two thousand years ago. But in God's spiritual and visionary plan, the Lamb killed before the world was created. What we see happening on the cross is the physical materialization of what had already been witnessed on the spiritual windows of heaven before time was made. This means that there is no future in God because today's future is already past in God's spiritual world. Whatever will happen to you tomorrow or next year, to God, it has already happened long ago. When it comes to the spiritual arena, time is suspended. God created time to redeem man. Time begins when God creates the earth, man, and the universe, for

He lives in eternity with no time. Time is mentioned in allusion or reference to the physical and material world.

For instance, in God's chronology, if we have to compare times, what is happening now for you isn't happening in Heaven. It happened long ago, even before you were born or before your parents and grandparents were born. God is too big, too brilliant, and too eternally existent. He is Jehovah - the self-existent One. He said to Moses, "I am that I am" (Exodus 3:14 KJV). He is greater than time and controls it.

Dear reader, what is happening to you today and now? There was already a program according to which you would be sitting there or standing there, reading this book. That is nothing new; it was already planned. "If that's so, apostle, then can I stay and do nothing because the end is already predestined and programmed?" Not necessarily, as we will learn in the coming chapters; there is a share for you in this process, something you must do to alter the program and script of events in the spiritual arena to conform to God's will for your life. A part of it is prayer.

Remember, you are a moral agent, endowed with free will to make choices, and for every choice, there are consequences - positive or negative. Therefore, you need to have spiritual discernment, be constantly filled with the Holy Spirit, and grow in spiritual intelligence through accurate knowledge of God's Word and will. Even King David said, "My frame was not hidden from you when I was made in the secret place when I was woven together in the depths of the earth. Your eyes saw my unformed body; all the days ordained for me were written in your book before one of them came to be" (Psalm 139:15-16 NIV).

Dear reader, the same applies to you too, because even when you were a mere embryo, God counted your bones; before your mother brought you into the world before your father met your mother, you were already born there in spirit. This is why if you don't understand the world and how it works, the devil can even manipulate this spirit world, and consequently, the man or woman you were supposed to marry ends up marrying the wrong person in the physical world. The devil can change things to the point where you find yourself in a marriage full of problems that seem endless. For example, for some people, there may be certain companies where they should be working, but the devil has manipulated things in the spirit world in such a way that he has put other individuals to work in their place. Someone can occupy a position that should be theirs, just by messing with the system in the spiritual arena, and out of nowhere, things that are logically-rationally inexplicable happen. There are people whose children should have been born already and yet were never born.

For instance, the angel Gabriel appeared to Mary and told her, "And behold, thou shalt conceive in thy womb, and bring forth a son, and you shalt call his name Jesus" (Luke 1:31 KJV). The information about Jesus' birth came to Mary when she didn't even think it would be possible to conceive without physical contact with her fiancé Joseph. Furthermore, when Jesus was born, angels appeared to the magi from the East and announced to them the birth of the King. In turn, the magi celebrated the news and went to worship baby Jesus with gifts. Note the angels' words, "Glory to God in the highest, and on earth peace, good will toward men" (Luke 2:14 KJV). Thus, there was a grand celebration in Heaven because, finally, humanity's suffering would come to an end, and the Kingdom of God would be installed in the hearts of men through Jesus. However, the devil didn't like the news, so he entered King Herod, who had all children from two years old and under killed. What was bothering him? The star of the child who was born King. Herod's soldiers were looking for that boy on whose shoulders the kingdom lay. Notice one thing: He was a boy who wasn't even walking yet, but someone from a great hierarchy on earth like Herod was seeking to kill him because he knew what he would become.

Chapter IV

What happens in the spiritual world when a prophecy is given

Dear reader, understand that the devil doesn't fight you for what you are today, but for what he knows you will be tomorrow. So, knowing your future, he fights you for that reason to destroy you. "How can he see?" you may ask. Simple - he sees through what God says. When God says something about someone, that is established in heaven, on earth, and in hell. So, the devil can see that there have been prophecies and words that have been spoken, spoken about you, and he does everything to make sure that it doesn't happen. Know that the devil is not omniscient; he doesn't know everything God knows, but he hears about a human being from the heavenly regions. In the spiritual arena, words are not mere acoustic sounds but visible, tangible, palpable objects; when spoken, those who operate in the spiritual world or are sensitive to it can automatically see the words moving in the process of materialization into the physical world. This is why the Scripture in Proverbs 18:21(NIV) says, " The tongue has the power of life and death, and those who love it will eat its fruit." Furthermore, Jesus emphasized the notion of the power of words when he said, "For by your words you will be acquitted, and by your words, you will be condemned" (Matthew 12:37 NIV).

Words play a predominant role in the spiritual arena, and as we will study later, they are elements of the spiritual world and modifying factors in the physical world. Many people have God's words pending over their lives still unfulfilled in the physical arena because they don't understand them. Jesus, explaining the parable of the sower to his disciples, said, "When anyone hears the message about the kingdom and does not understand it, the evil one comes and snatches away what was sown in their heart. This is the seed sown along the path" (Matthew 13:19 NIV). The term "snatches" denotes a quick action, often in the blink of an eye. It resembles that situation in which a bird flings itself into the sea to catch a fish in a short period. When does the devil come? When he has had glorious words spoken about you. That's why Paul said to Timothy, "Timothy, my son, I am giving you this command in keeping with the prophecies once made about you, so that by recalling them you may fight the battle well" (1 Timothy 1:18 NIV).

Do you understand now? When a prophecy is released, it often reveals God's plans or things that will happen on earth to a person or a nation. As such, these prophetic words provoke a reaction from the spirit world: on the one hand, God's angels, we can also call them "forces of good," are activated and sent to facilitate the fulfillment of God's words prophecies or promises. They are ministering spirits sent to serve on behalf of the heirs of salvation (Hebrews 1:14). What does this mean? Well, all those who are destined for salvation and those who are saved, God sends angels to assist, protect, and deliver them. However, these angelic activities or diplomatic missions of God's angels on behalf of men can only have legality and be effective when men pray. This is because prayer gives God the legal right or permission to intervene in the affairs of the earth. For example, for you, as a son or daughter of God, there are angels of God sent for your daily assistance in whatever situation you find yourself in. However, you must pray, or there must be someone praying for you, for them to come into action. The angelic intervention of light happens at the invitation of the human being through prayer.

Now, on the other hand, the angels of darkness, upon hearing that God has proclaimed something about you, try to fight you into giving up your faith and walking away. They have no power to prevent the fulfillment or movement of God's Word when He speaks. Still, they can provoke situations of discomfort until the individual who is about to receive or benefit from God's words becomes afraid, worried, or gives up his faith; until he moves his heart from the place where God's Word should land and germinate. This is called "spiritual warfare or spiritual battle" between the forces of good and evil for or against humanity. For this reason, prophecies must be used as weapons of war. When the devil has already messed with your life and tried to destroy everything you had or have, your last safe harbor is the Word of God: hold on to it, believe in it continually, and confess it over your life and the circumstances around you. The Word of God is lively and compelling, sharper, and more piercing than a two-edged sword. That is why it's called the "Sword of the Spirit" because it is the only effective weapon to defeat and destroy the evil plans against you.

Jesus said, "Heaven and earth shall pass away, but my words shall not pass away" (Matthew 24:35 KJV). Therefore, cling to God's Word. Believe that whoever remains firm in the Word of God will always return with a testimony, for he will be like a house built on the rock: come rain, flow rivers and/or blow winds, he will remain firm like Mount Zion - always unshakable. This is why Paul urged Timothy to use the prophecies spoken about him as weapons of warfare in his fight of faith. When a sign is given, it provokes spiritual reactions and stirs up spiritual warfare from the forces of darkness that try to delay or prevent its physical fulfillment.

Look at Jesus, ever since he was twenty-nine years old, we have no record of a severe temptation or attack by the devil. Likewise, we see no manifestation of him outside of what he had done through Herod. However, when Jesus reached the age of thirty - an age considered mature or senior by the Jews, he went to the Jordan River to be baptized by John the Baptist. The Heavens were opened, the Holy Spirit descended upon Him in the form of a dove, and a voice from heaven (Jehovah's voice) said, "This is My beloved Son, in whom I am well pleased." The Scripture narrates that Jesus was led into the desert to be tempted by the devil. And what was the main point of temptation? Jesus' identity, will, and character. And what was the object of attack against Jesus? The words that the Father had spoken over Him, "This is My beloved Son, in whom I am well pleased." Satan said, "If you are the Son of God, turn these stones into bread." Jesus knew that he was the Son of God, but he didn't yield his will to the devil's will but stood firm in his word.

Similarly, the devil can attack the believer's mind by accusing his faith in God, "If you truly are God's son or daughter, why haven't you gotten married, had a job or children by now?" If you don't understand

God's will revealed in the Holy Scriptures, you may give in to the devil. You must study the Word constantly and prayerfully.

For instance, how many brothers have received prophecies about their lives in the church? At first, things seemed to be fine, but everything started to get very complicated and almost difficult after the forecast. "Why does this happen, apostle?" - you may inquire. Well, because the devil wants you to abort the promise you have received from God. The devil is cunning and relentless (1 Peter 5:8).

Therefore, many brothers, for not having understood what to do after receiving a prophecy, cause this prophecy to fail. It's not fulfilled or doesn't materialize, and consequently, they end up blaming and accusing the man of God, calling him fake. The problem is that you haven't known how to receive or keep what God has given you. Dear reader, you must realize this. There is appropriate behavior and right attitudes for actions to be fully accomplished in the spiritual world. The battle is serious, and the strategies must be well defined.

God had planned that the people of Israel would go out of Egypt to Canaan - a land flowing with milk and honey. Wasn't that what He promised? The answer is yes, it was. So, did they all enter Canaan? No, not all entered because the Elders, due to constant rebellion, ingratitude, murmuring, and lack of faith, wandered in the wilderness for forty years and died. However, the original plan was that everyone would enter Canaan. Instead, only the youngest of those born out of Egypt, Caleb and Joshua, entered the promised land because they walked according to the instruction given by God for each moment.

Dear reader, when you don't walk according to God's instruction, you can receive a prophecy that is not fulfilled in your life. Things won't happen just because God has spoken, but because man has cooperated with Him by believing, praying, and confessing firmly.

For example, it's normal for me to say that I see an accident happening tomorrow; it actually happens; it's a prophecy. Why was I able to see it beforehand? Because I see in the spirit: I can see what is going to happen before it happens. But imagine I say, "I see an accident happening tomorrow at 10 am on road number 'X.'" After which, a group of brothers begins to pray to reverse what the devil has planned in the spirit and what God has seen and revealed to his servant. And suddenly, tomorrow at ten o'clock (10:00), no accident happens, but the prophecy has been recorded and posted on social media and/or television. Carnal people will say that Apostle Onório is fake. Why? Well, because they didn't understand that there were other spiritual laws triggered that reversed, neutralized, and/or canceled what was about to happen. The same can be seen concerning Herod when he wanted to kill the baby Jesus; how was the baby Jesus saved? The angel appeared to Joseph in a dream and said to him, "Get up, he said, take the child and his mother and escape to Egypt. Stay there until I tell you, for Herod is going to search for the child to kill him" (Matthew 2:13 NIV). Now, imagine the angel hadn't said that to Joseph or if Joseph hadn't acted on the instruction: fleeing to Egypt. It would have been fatal. Joseph escaped because he obeyed the instruction. The fleeing of Joseph and his wife Mary with the baby might look like a sign of weakness in the eyes of an immature Christian or the analysis of a carnal man; to us, the spiritual ones, we understand that it was an act of great wisdom on Joseph's part. He was obedient to God's voice and acted quickly. The Holy Scripture says, "The prudent see danger and take refuge, but the simple keep going and pay the penalty" (Proverbs 27:12 NIV). The King James Version says, " A prudent man foreseeth the evil, and hideth himself; but the simple pass on, and are punished." Do you understand? It takes wisdom to escape the devil's traps and crafty snares. Hearing God's voice and acting on it quickly is a sign of wisdom: it can save you from many evils and lousy company. I pray that God will give you a spirit of discernment and revelation. To choose to obey God's Word is to escape danger and guard yourself against making bad choices. God's Word never fails.

Sometimes, in counseling sessions, based on the Word of God, of course, I tell some sisters, "This relationship, which you are embarking on, has no future." Because they consider their feelings more than God's will, they move on and, consequently, start living in hellish homes. Sometime later, they come to me with their problems, but I had already warned them. The same has happened with men looking for women to marry. Why can I decipher God's will in this kind of situation or detect the misfortune of such stormy relationships? Because I see it in the spiritual world, and if you don't see, why can't you believe those who can see and are seeing?

It's like a scientist who uses special devices to make diagnoses in the health field, and he can see the cells in a person's blood, and he makes medical recommendations, but someone refutes and says that he doesn't see. Yes, you don't see the cells because you don't have the devices he has, but he has them, and he can see, so why can't you believe what he is saying, being that he has evidence?

Nowadays, science can tell how many months of pregnancy a woman has and can even see and tell the gender of the baby. How is this possible? Well, because there are devices that can penetrate the uterus, see, and take an X-ray, but to the average human eye, you can only look and see the belly growing and not have a general and precise notion of the pregnancy details.

As an example, before the birth of Prince, my first child, I told my wife the number of months, days, gender, and what that boy would be, long before he was born. Then, when she went to the appointment, the gynecologist did the ultrasound and gave her the same information I had already provided her. The gynecologist got this information from the scientific apparatus, and I got it from the prophetic anointing from the Holy Spirit. The Holy Spirit knows everything. The Holy Scripture in 1 Corinthians 2:11 (NIV) says, "For who knows a person's thoughts except their own spirit within them?

In the same way, no one knows the thoughts of God except the Spirit of God." This Scripture lets us know that the information about a being is located in his spirit. The Holy Spirit can penetrate man's spirit and gather all the information about him, including everything that has to do with his soul and body. God has used me in these dimensions too, but at the discretion of His Spirit, when and how He wants, depending on my sensitivity at that moment.

Another example is from our missionary's wife. Her husband called me saying that she was pregnant and asked for a spiritual ultrasound. He did it as if he knew God could use me to understand because he is a man of faith. I, being in Maputo, by the grace of God (praise Jesus' name) through the Holy Spirit, surrendered to the place where they were to do the ultrasound and then sent him a message. I told him it was a boy and gave him the characteristics, and the baby was born as per the description I had provided him through the phone. The details even included the boy's color because he is lighter in color than his mother and father. I told him the boy's color was so that the father wouldn't get frustrated and distrust his wife when the boy was born since the color was lighter than both of them. Of course, biologically, this can be explained due to the composition of the parents' genetic information and their ancestors. Nothing is impossible for our God.

The third example is of a sister who had been pregnant for eight months, and the doctor had told her it was a boy, but she wanted a girl. She came to one of our Heavenly Atmosphere services and asked for prayer. I prayed for her, by the power of God and the words I spoke over her, the Holy Spirit turned the boy into a girl, and a girl was born. How does this happen, and how can I handle these things and see changes happening in the physical from an intervention in the spirit? Simple, because I understand the spirit world; in it, things are manipulated. When we speak things, they materialize, becoming real.

If you are a sister reading this book and you haven't conceived or have infertility problems, I prophesy that you will conceive in the name of Jesus! Believe and receive your miracle now. All of this is a miracle because there are no natural laws to explain how this happens; it's by faith and the power of God. I have a vast repertoire of examples and testimonies, but I have only listed three occurrences to save time and words.

When you walk with God and understand the spiritual world, you discover that everything is possible; even what humanly seemed impossible.

I never forget the testimony of a sister who came to one of our services without a uterus. The doctor had removed it because she had had a pregnancy outside the womb, which was risky for her life. By a simple but anointed word, I prophesied, "there is a sister here without a uterus, but she is getting one now, in the name of Jesus, and she is going to conceive." She said she felt something moving in the area from where her uterus had been removed. Months later, she came to witness the birth of a baby boy. She became pregnant and gave birth to a boy. Her testimony is documented as proof that with God, anything is possible.

You know, when I pray for someone, and nothing happens, the strangest thing is: what is it about this person? What kind of heart does he have for the apostle to pray for him under God's anointing, and nothing happens? Probably, he must have hardened his heart not to receive. To receive your miracle, you will have to be converted and born again, or you will have to be more patient and wait on God.

CHAPTER V

Understanding the dichotomy of planes

The spiritual plane versus the material plane

Dear reader, understand that there is a spiritual and material plane, and things often don't happen in parallel. The physical- material world usually comes in tow, pulled, or attracted by the spiritual world. This revelation is potent. This is why before God does something for you here on earth today, he will first communicate it through his Word.

Notice this Bible passage, "And behold, in your womb, you will conceive and bear a son...". Do you see that the angel appeared and told Mary that she would give birth to a child? Well, this is an announcement coming from God's throne, announcing and preparing Mary of what would happen to her in the physical.

If you read the text of Matthew 1:22-23 (NIV), you notice the following, All this took place to fulfill what the Lord had said through the prophet: "The virgin will conceive and give birth to a son, and they will call him Immanuel" (which means "God with us").

The angel was announcing to Joseph something already told hundreds of years ago by the prophet Isaiah. But, unfortunately, there was a lapse of time between Isaiah's prophecy and its materialization.

Jesus grew up, was taken to the cross, and killed. When he was crucified, even the words he spoke on the cross had already been prophesied by David.

"Eli, Eli, lama sabactani; that is to say, My God, my God, why hast thou forsaken me?" (Matthew 27:46 KJV). David had spoken about this hundreds of years ago before Jesus physically came to earth. Remember the prophetic words of Isaiah, when he said, "Surely he took up our pain and bore our suffering, yet we considered him punished by God, stricken by him, and afflicted. But he was pierced for our transgressions, he was crushed for our iniquities; the punishment that brought us peace was on him, and by his wounds, we are healed" (Isaiah 53:4-5 NIV). Isaiah was looking at things from the spiritual plane: in the spirit world, or rather, in the heavenly places. How was this man able to say "we are healed" in reference to a person who had not yet been physically born on earth and whose biological mother had not yet been born? Isaiah spoke these words long before Mary or even her parents and grandparents were born.

Nevertheless, he said, "We are healed." How were we healed if the person who was to heal us had not yet been born into this world? What language or communication is that? He was speaking from a world, a sphere called the "spirit world," where things are not going to happen; they have already happened.

Therefore, God needed to move time to fulfill in the physical world what Isaiah had prophesied in the spiritual. Hundreds of years later, we see Jesus hanging on the cross and fulfilling in physical time, in the eyes of men and his disciples, what Isaiah had seen fulfilled in spirit hundreds of years before.

Looking at the text of 1 Peter 2:24 (NIV), we notice words similar to Isaiah's, but spoken now by an apostle who has seen, served, and walked with Jesus physically, saying, "And by his wounds, you have been healed." Now, Peter wasn't saying those words from the same perspective or plan as Isaiah. However, he told them from a physical standpoint because he had walked with Jesus and knew that Jesus Christ had already died on the cross and had ascended into Heaven, carrying in himself all the infirmities and pains of humanity. So, he said what happened in human chronological time. At the same time, Isaiah had vindicated this exact scenario by the spirit, telling what will happen in the spiritual world before it happens in the physical realm. He was a prophet, and prophets transcend the spirit into the spirit world, navigating it back and forth, going into the future and the past, and coming into the present. He wore a spiritual lens. This is why Paul said, "Consequently, you are no longer foreigners and strangers, but fellow citizens with God's people and also members of his household, built on the foundation of the apostles   and prophets, with Christ Jesus himself as the chief cornerstone" (Ephesians 2:19-20 NIV).

So, we see two men speaking of the same Jesus: Isaiah on the spiritual plane and Peter on the material plane, vindicating the information of his fellow servant Isaiah. Isaiah spoke of Christ, saying "we are healed" in reference to what had happened in God's sight and revealed to his servants, the prophets. On the other hand, Peter used the past perfect tense, "you have been healed," but in allusion to what had physically happened and witnessed by many people. Peter used the time of men, and Isaiah used the time of angels and the spirits of the glorified righteous, both speaking of the same incident. On the one hand, we have Isaiah's spiritual truth, and on the other hand, we have Peter's material truth. However, spiritual truth always precedes physical reality and leads the latter to its trailer, as if it were a leash or carriage. Therefore, anyone who definitely wants to change something he doesn't like in life on the physical- material plane should first do so in the spirit. If a person is blessed in the spirit and is aware of that blessing, he will enjoy it physically; but if someone is cursed in the spirit, nothing he does physically will work until he changes the spirit world through words and spiritual laws. So, the spiritual world plays a dominant and influential role in the physical realm because time doesn't exist there.

Dear reader, do you now understand the need to believe in and master the spiritual world? How many beautiful women still cannot get a husband to marry them because a demon considers himself their spiritual husband and barring their sentimental happiness? No hair salon or cosmetic products will make her appreciated and married before a higher power liberates her than the demons in the spiritual world. How many men try to start a project and never finish it, and even with academic qualifications, don't get good jobs and stable life? There are even certain situations where a demon can bar a person's academic advancement, preventing him from finishing a course, giving him laziness, demoralizing him from writing his monograph, thesis, or dissertation. What is the solution? One must break through these limitations and remove these hindrances in the spiritual arena. Once the impediment is removed, the whole endeavor will succeed.

When Isaiah spoke about Christ's death, his contemporaries probably thought he was paranoid, a madman, because they didn't see it from his perspective. Prophets live in their spiritual territories and have certain extra prerogatives because they have had their spirits enlightened, eyes unveiled, and ears sharpened/enhanced to see, hear, and move in the spiritual world for the sake of the people and God's plans. And here is one who writes this book you are reading now. Prophets are commanders of spiritual territories and are heavily garrisoned and protected. Hence, natural men don't understand them when they speak. Religious people persecute them, accusing them of falsehood and heresy because their understanding and spiritual vision are *sui-generis* and out of this world; they see words when others only hear them. This is one of the reasons why prophetic ministries are so persecuted and misunderstood because they do significant damage to the kingdom of darkness and the devil's evil plans.

It's a blessing to have a prophet in your life. You can benefit from protection and particular graces just by being under one of these covers. What covers you? The sphere of spiritual influence that the prophet carries and the spiritual jurisdiction of his superintendence and vigilance over a physical territory in which he stands. This is why Elisha cried out, "My father, my father, chariots of Israel and their horsemen," referring to Elijah as he was being raptured into heaven, alive. What are these chariots? Spiritual chariots of fire, war chariots for spiritual battles. What are these horsemen? They are angels of God, war angels at the disposal of the trigger of the prophet's word, which comes out of the barrel [of the mouth] of the prophet. They fight on behalf of God's people and carry blessings and prosperity to them when the prophet prays. Therefore, it's very dangerous to persecute prophets. Even fire fell from the sky and consumed a hundred soldiers who wanted to arrest Elijah, and bears came out of nowhere, out of the field, and consumed the young men who harassed the prophet Elisha by calling him bald.

Even in Jesus' time, when Peter took out a sword and cut off Malchus' ear, servant of the high priest at the moment he had come with Judas and some soldiers, Jesus said, "Put your sword in its place; for all who take the sword to the sword will die. Or do you think that I could not now pray to my Father and that He would not give me more than twelve legions of angels? But how then shall the Scriptures be fulfilled, which say that thus it must be?" With these words, Jesus wanted to assure Peter that:

1. It wasn't necessary to physically fight in this battle;

2. His being arrested wasn't a mere demonstration of weakness, but for the fulfillment of the Scripture, the divine script prescribed in the heavenly annals;

3. He would pray, and the Father would send eighty- two thousand (over 80,000) angels to defend him and fight for him.

Can you imagine that many angels defending Jesus? If even one angel could only kill one hundred and eighty-five thousand (185000) valiant Assyrian soldiers, and their king Sennacherib fled in defeat and was later killed by his sons! From night to daytime, they were just bodies lying on the ground, killed by just one angel who had come to protect God's people in answer to the prayer of the prophet Isaiah and King Hezekiah. As one of Pastor Janifer Cutane's song verses says, "God is great and eternal; his power never fails."

Dear reader, trusting in this God and His power to protect, guard, and guide you, you can say, as one of the stanzas of this song, "Crying Lasts a Night" by Pastor Janifer says, "You will be my God, forever, you will be my God forever, you will be my God forever." Yes, He is faithful.

Dear reader, you must look at life from the spiritual perspective, as-suring yourself of spiritual truths and not be moved by observable and sensible facts. The Word of God has never failed, never fails, and will never fail. It is faithful. Therefore, believe in it regardless of apparent circumstances or contrary voices; it always prevails. Heaven and earth will pass away, but it will never pass away.

For example, it's normal and common for me to come up to someone and say, "Congratulations, great businessman!" The person looks at their current condition and thinks it's not true. They don't see themselves as God sees them in the spirit, in the light of the lens of His Word. What I'm saying may sound absurd and unbelievable, but I'm saying it from a higher perspective than their current condition; I'm speaking from a world I'm in: the spiritual world.

Similarly, I can come up and say to a sister, "Congratulations on your marriage, sister," even though I know she has no fiancé or comes from a family with marital problems and marriage difficulties. Or I can even tell her, "Your three children are blessed," even though I know she has fibroids and cannot conceive. In all of this, realize that I'm speaking from an objective perspective, telling you God's mind and His view of your situation. It's up to you to believe, receive, and create an expectation for the materialization of God's plans and will. As Mary said, "Behold the handmaid of the Lord; be it unto me according to thy word" (Luke 1:38 KJV).

Therefore, you may be facing challenges, barriers, and problems in the physical world, while in the spiritual arena, it's only a matter of time; right now, God is adjusting things here on earth to conform to His eternal heavenly plan. For that reason, you need to abide by God's Word. As the Scripture attests, "Your word, LORD, is eternal; it stands firm in the heavens" (Psalm 119:89 NIV). That's right, forever.

CHAPTER VI

The power of words

The word of God: the modifier of things in the spiritual and physical arena

The Word of God is the modifier of things on earth. There is what in linguistics is called a modifier, and it has an adjectival value because it attributes qualities and describes names, and nouns, characterizing them.

For example:

When a baby is born, it's delivered with no name, attributes, no identity, and almost nothing. In practice, up to this point, there is no modifier describing it. What happens then? Someone observes him or sees him for the first time and says: he is light, or dark, tall, or short, firm, or weak. Light, dark, tall, short, strong, and weak are adjectives and modify something about him, describing his characteristics and traits. These nominal modifiers make it so that he understands what he didn't know he was growing up.

The Word of God works in the same way: It changes our lives, creates things in the spiritual arena, and brings them into the physical arena by the agency of the Holy Spirit's power. When He says something about an individual, He describes his real identity, what he has, and what he is in the spirit. It's in the spirit where we see the natural beauty of someone and what he is worth to God and other people. Natural human eyes cannot uncover this beauty because they have been corrupted by the fall of Adam and are, therefore, limited by nature and are opened when the man is born again and receives the Holy Spirit.

Dear reader, if God says that you are strong, rich, blessed, and healed and protected, believe it, and condition your mind and speech according to this report from Him. God won't do anything on earth that His Word hasn't announced. God's Word changes circumstances, and when a man believes in it, God turns what seemed impossible into a possibility.

A practical example is summarized in the story of Gideon, the judge and military liberator of Israel. With him, we can understand two perspectives: the divine or spiritual, from which God and the angels saw him in heaven and the highest heaven, and the human vision, in which he himself lived, limited and miserable. God sent him a message, a word that would characterize him, and if he believed it and looked at his life in the light of that word, he would be an overcomer - a champion for his people. So the angel of the Lord appeared to Gideon and said to him, "The LORD is with you, mighty warrior... Go in the strength you have and save Israel out of Midian's hand. Am I not sending you?" "Pardon me, my lord," Gideon replied, "but how can I save Israel? My clan is the weakest in Manasseh, and I am the least in my family." The Lord answered, "I will be with you, and you will strike down all the Midianites, leaving none alive" (Judges 6:12,14-16 NIV).

It all happened when harvest time came: the Midianites invaded the land of Israel and stole all the harvest and livestock of the people of Israel, plundering them and sowing hunger everywhere. At this time, the whole world was afraid and terrified of these imposing and merciless invaders.

Gideon, however, was threshing wheat when the angel of the Lord appeared to him and spoke to him. The angel came with a report in the form of words, describing this great leader who still had his eyes closed to this spiritual reality, "The LORD is with you a mighty warrior." Mighty means brave, strong and fearless. First, the angel of the Lord assures him of God's presence with him, bringing this lost awareness of Israel that the Lord, their God, was with them. However, Gideon looked at himself and saw himself as weak, poor, and vulnerable, but the angel of the Lord looked at him and said that he was strong.

In fact, from God's perspective, Gideon could single-handedly smite all the Midianites simultaneously as if he were fighting with just one man. This was the way God saw Gideon's strength and military abilities, but he didn't understand this and needed supernatural signs and evidence to be convinced. The angel was patient and gave him the signs he asked for, but he still didn't believe because he was too afraid and thought he was incapable. He needed a modifier for his transformation from fearful to brave. He was already courageous in spirit, but his physical stature atrophied and conditioned his victorious potential.

He led a large army, but God made rules in which the overwhelming majority were disqualified, and only three hundred men were considered fit to accompany Gideon into battle. Even so, he remained fearful and hesitant to take steps toward God's calling to free the people from Midianite oppression.

Now, everything changed when he went to the Midianites' camp. When he was there, he heard two Midianites talking, and one of them was telling his companion about the dream he had had during the night, "I had a dream," he was saying. "A round loaf of barley bread came tumbling into the Midianite camp. It struck the tent with such force that the tent overturned and collapsed." His friend responded, "This can be nothing other than the sword of Gideon son of Joash, the Israelite. God has given the Midianites and the whole camp into his hands" (Judges 7:13-14 NIV)

Hearing these words from the Midianites' camp, Gideon gained courage, attacked them, and defeated them. But it took him a long time to understand something so simple and become convinced of God's voice.

Dear reader, you are strong inside, believe it. When God says you are strong, believe it; when He says you are blessed, believe it. When He says you are healed, believe it; when He says your suffering is over, believe it. Agree with God because His report never fails. He is speaking from a perspective where things are not going to happen; they have already happened. It's up to you to take hold of God's words and modify your life accordingly, based on what they say about you.

This spiritual world is more real than the physical one you are in, and a single word can change everything; it is a sphere of spiritual activities. It is a dynamic world. Right now, as you are reading this book, people are getting married. There are people signing contracts. There are women giving birth and others getting engaged. People are graduating. A lot of activities are going on right now. But these people can have these blessings stolen by the devil and the demons if they don't know the Word of God and take possession of what belongs to them in Christ - reclaiming it by faith in the blood of Jesus.

By the grace God has given me, I provide you with this information so that in your spirit, you can access the materialization of God's plans in your life without diabolical interference. It will be up to you to assume the position in which Christ has placed you. You believe, and it happens, and if you don't, nothing will happen. Remember, God has already blessed you with all the spiritual blessings in the heavenly places. It is up to you to take possession of them. This is why the Scripture says, "Through knowledge the righteous escape" (Proverbs 11:9 NIV).

For example, every day when I wake up in the morning, I usually know where I will go, who I will meet, what will happen, and how that day.

What often happens is that I have to work hard in the spirit to change certain things - changing them by the word. For instance, I may decide that there is a certain kind of people that I shouldn't meet this week and not come my way.

There are Divine Helpers, who are people that God puts on our path to be a blessing to us in every phase of our life until the day we leave this earth. He has already planned how your life will be and has placed all the right people along the way; you just have to pray and ask the Holy Spirit for help. Sometimes, God will recognize you as a blessing to other people as well. He can use you to bless someone.

When you wake up in the morning, tune into God's channel by prayer and meditation on His Word and align yourself with the Word and the Spirit of God. He will cause you to meet the people you should meet, do what you should do, go where you should go, speak what you should talk, have what you should have, be where you should be, and be what you should be in that day and time.

No wonder David said, "He makes me lay down in green pastures, he leads me beside quiet waters.... Surely your goodness and love will follow me all the days of my life" (Psalm 23:2,6 NIV). David knew how to schedule his day and prepare for his victories. He was a spiritual man.

We can notice the same thing with Elijah. At the time when there was a famine of three and a half years, the word of God came to Elijah, instructing him, "Leave here, turn eastward and hide in the Kerith Ravine, east of the Jordan. You will drink from the brook, and I have directed the ravens to supply you with food there" (1 Kings 17:3-4 NIV)

God instructed Elijah to make a migratory movement from a physical place, and if he had not obeyed by leaving that place, he would have had no food.

There are times when you have to physically move around to fit God's time, plan, and purposes.

This is why certain people, even though God so loves them, if they had not gone to church, certain good things would not have happened to them.

His obedience saved Elijah from God's word.

When he arrived at the stream of Kerith and found himself where God wanted him to be physical, the ravens brought him bread and meat. Can you see how God is? God knew that Elijah didn't like vegetables, and in order not to give him a hard time, the meat arrived prepared and ready to be eaten by the prophet-man of God.

When the water of the brook of Kerith was exhausted, the word of the LORD came again to give him new instructions as to his survival to the world crisis. Thus, the Scripture says, "Then the word of the Lord came to him: "Go at once to Zarephath in the region of Sidon and stay there. I have directed a widow there to supply you with food" (1 Kings 17:8-9 NIV)

When he got there, he found a woman who was also hungry; having only a handful of flour and a bit of oil. So, he blessed them, and they multiplied. Thus, while the famine was ravaging the region and the entire neighborhood, this woman's house had inexhaustible food because the word of the Lord was with Elijah, and he had prophesied about the oil and the flour, guaranteeing their multiplication and perpetuity.

This is yet another demonstration of God's power and provisioning love for His children and servants. No one should suffer or be in need.

King David said, "The young lions do lack and suffer hunger, but they that seek the Lord shall not want any good thing" (Psalm 34:10 KJV). This was the man who, at the end of his life, said, "I have been young, and now am old; yet have I not seen the righteous forsaken, nor his seed begging bread" (Psalm 37:25 KJV).

Dear reader, understand that your life was made for the glory of God; it should not be full of these scars that you have, but it should be a sweet, good, and glorious life. Why have many believers not had this glorious experience? Because most cannot hear God when He speaks, they follow more the voice, the pleasures, and the desires of the flesh, and consequently, go into the pit. Everyone should be able to follow the voice of the Holy Spirit, the Word of God, walk in green pastures, and be led meekly, not aggressively or tumultuously, but gently into quiet waters. This way, they wouldn't be frustrated but would have their souls cooled with peace - the peace of God that surpasses all understanding I discovered this a long time ago. That's why I like to teach teens and young adults to grow up with this kingdom mindset and culture and have a sweet and glorious life - a life of constant victories. Glory to God!

In short: On the one hand, there is a spiritual world where plans are made to happen in the physical world. But, on the other hand, there is a physical world in which we live now, where things happen day by day, things planned in the spiritual world to occur in the physical world.

For our success in life, we need to understand this spiritual world to align ourselves with it in terms of understanding it and knowing what to do to avoid and cancel certain things that we don't want to see happen, which are the devil's work. However, we also need to use the authority that Christ has given us to enforce those things that are consistent with our well-being according to God's good will expressed in His Word. This is why Jesus said, "I will give you the keys of the kingdom of heaven; whatever you bind on earth will be bound in heaven, and whatever you loose on earth will be loosed in heaven" (Matthew 16:19 NIV).

Keys represent principles, the knowledge that makes God's Kingdom work. To turn on means to permit, and to turn off means to forbid. You have that authority for effect by using your tongue - of the Word by faith and communion with Jesus.

Here are some of the keys: use them. There is power in your tongue.

SAY Spiritual world, spiritual arena. Hallelujah.

Chapter VII

The power of dreams

Amplify your dreams' horizons

Dreams can change things in the spiritual and physical arena. When I speak of dreams, I don't mean the succession of images in the form of a short or long film when you sleep. Those are also very important, but they are independent of you and not in your control; you can only cancel the ones you don't like and pray for the ones that are in accordance with God's will for your life

Dreams are modifiers of things in the spirit world.

"Dreams" here represent the soul's desire imprinted by the Holy Spirit as a way to lead it to a better and glorious life. So, the Scripture attests, "For it is God who works in you to will and to act in order to fulfill his good purpose" (Philippians 2:13 NIV). God wants you to be imbued with dreams – dreams of good things and a good life for yourself and others. This doesn't come from the devil but God, and He often places this desire within your spirit. To do so, He gives you will and then gives you grace, a power that enables you to achieve those dreams

Moreover, it was the LORD himself who said, "For I know the plans I have for you, declares the LORD; plans to prosper you and not to harm you, plans to give you hope and a future" (Jeremiah 29:11 NIV). Notice that God has good thoughts concerning your life. Often, He places these thoughts/plans within the man's heart and incubates them by the Holy Spirit - giving meaning to your life on this earth. You have to dream because your future can be created through dreams and words. There is much that is glorious that you have not yet seen or experienced: levels of divine glory and success. There is always more in God. In Him, there is an infinity of glorious things to achieve. That is why He wants you to grow from faith to faith and glory to glory, hallelujah!

Notice this Scripture, "However, as it is written, what no eye has seen, what no ear has heard, and what no human mind has conceived"— the things God has prepared for those who love him" (1 Corinthians 2:9 NIV). What glorious things has God prepared for you, dear reader? Things that this world has not yet seen, nor do you have any idea how they might materialize. So, don't be afraid to dream big - God-sized dreams. Dreams that will require special grace from God to achieve. Your task is to dream according to God's will and purpose for your life. "How can I know, apostle?" Simple, verse 10 of the previous chapter explains, "These are the things God has revealed to us by his Spirit. The Spirit searches all things, even the deep things of God." You must spend time studying and meditating on God's Word. It's essential and indispensable that you spend time with God in prayer because, this way, your spirit will be made fruitful with the Word of God that will program you for a life of success and glory. The Spirit will enlighten your heart, and the faith in God's Word will be strong, and whatever you dream, conceive, and say will come to pass. Dream and dream big. A vision of God's will is not an illusion or mirage; it's a panoramic picture captured by your spirit and mind in contact with God's purpose revealed in His Word for you.

So, broaden your view of things and adapt, constantly reinventing yourself in the molding process by God's Word: always renewing the way you think and the object of your thoughts. What a man thinks conditions what he is.

Don't let the seemingly negative and disadvantageous conditions and circumstances in which you were born, limit your potential or condition your future. You can overcome and transcend human limitations through faith in God's Word and dreams, and through your mouth, you can create a better world for yourself, your family, and others. Refuse to be labeled as poor, miserable, sick, cursed, and defeated. You are an overcomer in Christ Jesus. The Scripture states,

"In all these things we are more than conquerors through him who loved us" (Romans 8:37 NIV).

God's Word is clear about our spiritual position and advantage in Christ: "Praise be to the God and Father of our Lord Jesus Christ, who has blessed us in the heavenly realms with every spiritual blessing in Christ" (Ephesians 1:3 NIV).

Dear reader, understand that things are not going to happen; they have already happened. You have to learn to look at yourself in the light of God's Word: it is real; it does not fail. It is the mirror that emits and reflects precisely what you are in the spirit. This is why I said that whoever does not listen to God's Word and does not do what it says will never be fully happy in this world.

Now, when it says, "With all spiritual blessings," they are spiritual because, in the spirit, things are spiritual and not material. Therefore, one must understand that spiritual things come first, and they are molds of material things.

A mold is a shape from which something is created or made. Consider, for instance, that you want to make a thousand cakes from a mold; a thousand cakes will look alike because they will be coming out of the same mold. So, what you are physically is a result of what you are in the spirit.

There was a young fisherman who went fishing next to an older man, also a fisherman. While the two were fishing, the young man was lucky enough to catch many fish, enormous in size. Whenever he caught a big fish, he would throw it overboard, and when he caught a small fish, he would put it in his fisherman's bag.

The older fisherman was watching all of this. And it amazed him because the young man was wasting an opportunity to have lots of fish, and big. So, perplexed, he approached the young fisherman and asked him why he threw them overboard every time he found big fish. The young man said he threw the big fish overboard because he only had a small frying pan in his house, and he had nowhere to fry the big fish because it wouldn't fit.

What that young man needed was a big frying pan. When he caught the big fish, he should have gone home and changed/molded the pan, enlarging it; but he let the small pan condition his mind and dictate his attitudes

The spiritual world conditions the physical world. The young man's vision was too small. He had the opportunity to go beyond, but he didn't because he thought small. He didn't dream big.

How many people today are like that young man? They waste time and opportunities; they don't give value and meaning to everything good that God puts in their way, whether in the form of opportunities, things, or people.

Why do we teach the Word? So that your eyes will be opened to understand and then take your position of dominion in Christ. Release the dreams of God that are in you. Change the circumstances around you. Write those dreams down and do something for them. God helps those who, by faith, do something, taking steps forward in obedience. Where would you like to see changes: in your marriage, family, job, studies, ministry, country, neighborhood, business? Dream and do something!

Chapter VIII

Understanding the concept of the Heavenly places

"In the heavenly places" (Ephesians 6:12 NKJV).

The word "heavenly places" is derived from the Greek "*Epouranios*," meaning "sphere of spiritual activities." In this sphere, activities take place, actions are carried out, plans are drawn up, and things happen there. Daily and permanently, there are activities taking place in the spiritual sphere, that is, in the heavenly places. What are these activities? They are spiritual activities that roughly influence people's circumstances, life, and behavior here on earth. However, because people don't understand that this spiritual world exists, they become victims of the devil's negative actions perpetrated from this spiritual sphere

Heavenly places don't refer to Heaven

You must understand that when we speak of heavenly places, we don't mean heaven, where God's throne is. There are several layers or dimensions of heaven. For example, Paul speaks of the third heaven, where he was taken when he encountered Jesus and given a gospel to preach to the Gentiles. It was in this dimension where Paul first received visions and revelations. Look at the report he provides, "I must go on boasting. Although there is nothing to be gained, I will go on to visions and revelations from the Lord. I know a man in Christ who fourteen years ago was caught up to the third heaven…[he] was caught up to paradise and heard inexpressible things, things that no one is permitted to tell" (2 Corinthians 12:1-4 NIV). Other versions translate the word "paradise" as "third heaven," and that is where Paul was taken in spirit.

He must have gone into a trance, where there was a suspension of his human faculties, and his spirit transcended into heaven, outside his body. Finding himself in this dimension, he was instructed, trained, and equipped for the work of the ministry by Jesus Christ – his Lord.

In two thousand and twelve, I also remember that I was taken up in spirit to the third heaven and given words to eat in the form of a scroll, which I was to preach to the nations, languages, and people of the earth. I also went into a spiritual trance; I had a rapture of the senses. The Lord Jesus taught me so much that there is no vocabulary of human language that can summarize and teach everything. That is why I have so much information to pass on, but I think that there are things that I will never be able to teach to exhaustion due to the load of revelations that I received in the third heaven

When you reach that dimension, you are given a different perspective on life and the world. To this day, I have in my spirit, in my heart, the scroll of information and revelations that I received. I'm conscious of it. Many people who follow my ministry are fascinated by miracles and, unfortunately, outline Apostle Onório only in miracles. However, my strong point is the Word's teaching because I have a scroll of revelations inside me and, every time I open my mouth to speak, the words spontaneously emanate from me. Just as Jesus said, "Out of his belly shall flow rivers of living water" (John 7:38 KJV), referring to the outpouring of the Holy Spirit. This is how I feel: graced and loved by Jesus, my Lord. Miracles and signs are like the icing on the cake that vindicates and support my ministry, but I have been sent to save souls through anointed words, accompanied by signs and wonders.

When we talk about heavenly places, we are not referring to Heaven because the image that many have of the word "Heaven" is summed up as the place where God is seated on his throne.

In Heaven, where God's throne is, no demons enter. Therefore, the activities that take place in Heaven are not the same as in heavenly places. The only activities that happen in Heaven and are beneficial to God are the praise and worship of Him and the daily reports He receives from the angels.

Understand that when we speak of days, hours, months, years, centuries, or millennia, we use these expressions from the perspective of time in the physical world, not the spiritual, because in the spiritual arena, there is no time. That is why only spirits walk their class in these layers. Enoch and Elijah, who were captured alive, had their bodies and souls glorified along with Moses so that they could ascend and continue to live in Heaven until today without having had their bodies buried. This is why the Holy Bible speaks of the righteous spirits being glorified and elevated, thus qualifying them to have an eternal covering over the temporal body and an incorruptible covering over the corruptible body (See Hebrews 12:23).

CHAPTER VIII

Angelic activities versus demonic activities

In the heavenly places, some activities influence life here on earth. For instance, there are angelic activities, which are activities done by angels. Did you know that angels patrol the earth daily and then go to heaven and report back to God? The prophet Zechariah saw this: angels patrolling the earth every day and giving God a report on how the earth is doing. So, there is angelic activity going on in the heavenly places. Look at Zechariah's description, "During the night I had a vision, and there before me was a man mounted on a red horse. He was standing among the myrtle trees in a ravine. Behind him were red, brown, and white horses. I asked, "What are these, my lord?" The angel who was talking with me answered, "I will show you what they are." Then the man standing among the myrtle trees explained, "They are the ones the Lord has sent to go throughout the earth." And they reported to the angel of the Lord who was standing among the myrtle trees, "We have gone throughout the earth and found the whole world at rest and in peace" (Zechariah 1:8-11 NIV).

There are several types of angels, and they don't all look alike; they don't all have the same appearance and function. This is because angels are not a race, like humans and animals. They are creatures, and each creature differs from the other. This is why sometimes we read about angels with an ox face, others with a lion face, and others with an eagle face, and so on. The angel also can incarnate and appear in physical form to the humans to whom he has been sent. For example, the angels who went with the LORD to visit Abraham and announce to him the destruction of Sodom and Gomorrah took on a physical form. This phenomenon is usually called "angelophany," the physical appearance of angels in human form. But their nature and habitation are not human, for the earth was given to the man with a physical body. The two angels left the LORD talking to Abraham as they went to Sodom and Gomorrah with fire and brimstone to destroy them. Alone, they set fire to the two wicked and sinful cities when Lot and his daughters had already left. These were angels of war and destruction.

Angels have various missions: there are angels of war sent by God to protect and fight for the saints, and their captain is the Archangel Michael, as we will see later. There are angels of prosperity and good news, like Archangel Gabriel, angels of healing, like Archangel Raphael, who doesn't appear in the canonical books but is a principality of God. In addition to typology, there is also a hierarchy among angels. There are angels with more authority and prerogatives than others. No wonder that Archangel Michael came to Gabriel's aid when the latter had been hindered by the prince of Persia when he was going to answer Daniel, who had been in prayer for twenty-one days. There are thousands and thousands of angels. The Scripture confirms, "But you have come to Mount Zion, to the city of the living God, the heavenly Jerusalem. You have come to thousands upon thousands of angels" (Hebrews 12:22 NIV).

When you are born again, God assigns you an angel to walk with you and carry your prayers to Heaven. You are overprotected. If you saw the protection you have in the spirit, and the angels who daily fight for you, your outlook on life would be different. For me, this is clearer because God has given me the grace not only to understand the spirit world but also to navigate it and see the angels and their operations on earth.

Also, understand that angels and cherubim are not the same species. Angels have usually attributed wings, but it is the cherubim who, roughly speaking, have wings. One of the major functions of cherubim is to protect; hence we can call them guardian cherubim. They offer enormous protection to God's people when they camp with you. Most of them are in Heaven, some around the throne of God, and have different kinds of faces, including man faces.

God's angels patrol the earth, send answers and good news to God's children, and serve for the benefit of the saints. They can prevent air, land, and sea accidents whenever demons want to drink human blood in large quantities or when someone who wants to enrich himself by making pacts with the devil points out unknown people or family members who should die as a sacrifice. Also, they protect God's people and humanity in general from wizards and various kinds of evil. In addition to their protective function, some even bring blessings and open doors of prosperity to the people of God. At this moment, as you read this book, there is a great work carried out by God's angels. They go up to Heaven and come down to earth. There are even angels who come to take the spirits of the saints to Heaven when their days on earth are already fulfilled. But some demons and angels take the impious to hell. There are angels whose mission is to kill the persecutors of God's people.

CHAPTER IX

How to activate the angelical activities in your and humanity's favor

One of the greatest ways to activate the work of angels is prayer. It's not a coincidence that Jesus taught us the duty to pray always and never faint (Luke 18:1 NIV). Verse 7 says, "And will not God bring about justice for his chosen ones, who cry out to him day and night? Will he keep putting them off?" He overemphasizes here the importance and necessity of praying. But to pray in faith. That's why verse 8 says, "I tell you, he will see that they get justice, and quickly. However, when the Son of Man comes, will he find faith on the earth?"

We read in the Holy Scriptures countless times in which angels are sent to protect God's people in answer to their constant and continuous prayers. You may get impatient and think that God's response to your prayers is delayed. This delay is not God's deafness to your requests, but it may be due to a battle that God and his army are fighting in the spirit for your benefit as well as your family's benefit. Have bold faith and arm yourself with great patience. Spiritual struggles and battles are real but rest in God's power, love, and faithfulness.

When King Sennacherib of Assyria came to take the kingdom of Judah into captivity; Isaiah, the prophet, and King Hezekiah prayed to Heaven for help. In response, God sent an angel who, in just one night, killed one hundred and eighty-five thousand strong men of the Assyrian army, leading to their defeat and to abort their plan. So, we see here, in this context, the activity of one angel.

When Peter was arrested, and Herod wanted to kill him with the sword, the Church prayed continually to God for him. In answer, God sent an angel who freed Peter from prison and killed King Herod, the enemy of the Gospel and men of God.

Angels are real, and they are among us now. There are more angels on earth now than the number of human beings because the battles against humanity are so intense that no flesh would be saved if they didn't intervene. Satan would like to annihilate all mankind in one day. But he cannot do it because of the saints' prayers and the church. That is why he hates the Church and encourages rulers to enact laws against God's work. But we have to pray to stop all the devil's plans as our brothers and sisters in the Early Church did. They proved to us that with continuous prayer, we can neutralize the demons' activity and all the devil's evil plans against humanity: against the church and human families.

Why do we have to pray? Because the earth was given to man — with a physical body, and spirits are not legal on earth without man's permission and legal invitation by prayer. Therefore, you must pray when things don't seem to go well and pray when things go well. You must pray without ceasing. Paul, a man, specialized in spiritual matters, with credentials of having gone to the third heaven, urged, "Pray without ceasing" (1 Thessalonians 5:17). Never stop praying, and especially, pray based on the Word of God, reinforcing that His will be done on earth, as it is in Heaven.

Here are other exhortations, "I exhort therefore, that, first of all, supplications, prayers, intercessions, and giving of thanks, be made for all men; For kings, and for all that are in authority; that we may lead a quiet and peaceable life in all godliness and honesty. For this is good and acceptable in the sight of God our Saviour; Who will have all men to be saved, and to come unto the knowledge of the truth" (1 Timothy 2:1-4 KJV).

Life is spiritual, so faith, prayer, and communion with God are practically indispensable because there will be almost no divine intervention to help men unless they pray for each other.

CHAPTER X

Demonic activities

Heavenly places are, as we defined earlier, spheres of spiritual activity that influence the lives of human beings on earth. We study the activity of God's angels that ascend and descend on earth, fulfilling their duties and tasks on behalf of God's people and ensuring that God's will is done on earth. These are the forces of good and light, struggling on behalf of humanity and activated by the incessant prayers of the saints, who day and night ascend to God like incense.

However, in addition to the angelic activities of good and light, there are also demonic activities going on in the heavenly places. It's in the heavenly places that accidents are planned to happen on earth. Also, it's in the heavenly places that deaths are planned to happen on earth. All of this happens in the spirit world or spiritual arena. My prayer and heart's desire is that God will open your understanding to recognize these spiritual realities and the operations of these antagonistic forces.

Paul exhorts, "For we do not wrestle against flesh and blood, but against principalities, against powers, against the rulers of the darkness of this age, against spiritual hosts of wickedness in the heavenly places" (Ephesians 6:12 NKJV).

This Bible passage reveals to us the antagonistic forces and tormentors against which we have to fight. First of all, we must keep in mind that this battle is not physical but spiritual, and it actually takes place in the heavenly places, also called "high and superhuman regions." Since this is a battle between light and darkness, and its field is the mind and the heavenly places, we must also use weapons suitable for this kind of battle - spiritual and not carnal armor. In parallel, the Scripture in 2 Corinthians 10:3-4 (NIV) says, "For though we live in the world, we do not wage war as the world does. The weapons we fight with are not the weapons of the world. On the contrary, they have divine power to demolish strongholds." This text makes us understand that although we live inside this physical body (flesh), eat, work, study and perform daily activities like any human being, we are literally in a battle. For this one, our weapons are not carnal but spiritual because the enemy is also spiritual.

Often, demons and spiritual hosts of wickedness can (by finding an opening) influence a once loving husband and turning him into someone who acts like an animal, or a woman who minutes ago was docile and meek, into an aggressive person exhibiting inhuman behavior. What can you do in these circumstances? First, pray for that person and rebuke the evil spirit that influenced him, "In the name of Jesus, you, spirit of darkness, take your claws out of my husband, or my wife, now and come back no more." You don't need to do this with him or her listening; you can find a quiet place to pray and, even from a distance, rebuke the evil spirit, and with a word, it will go away, and there will be harmony at home. Second, suppose your children are the ones exhibiting bad behavior. In that case, you can break the influence of these dark spirits with a word, "You, principality of darkness behind my children's negative behavior, under the blood of Christ and in the name of Jesus, I break your influence over them now. Let go of them and set them free, in the name of Jesus." You will see substantial changes when these spirits' influence is removed.

If you don't understand the spiritual world and how it influences relationships, you can consequently lead to physical aggression and end up in prison unnecessarily. Know that life is spiritual, and we have to treat it spiritually as well.

It's in the heavenly places where it's planned - how, when, under what circumstances - a pregnant woman should lose that pregnancy when someone loses their husband or wife. There are strategies laid out as to how and when someone on earth should lose their job or when their business should fail. After these plans have matured, the dark spirits seek physical "agents" through which these plans will be carried out. What for? So that men and newspapers will accuse the bus driver or the driver of the car that crashed, the psychological problems of the driver, or mechanical failures of the car. These mechanical failures and other reasons have a demon influencing behind them. But how do you place blame on a spirit that you don't see? Simple, the problem is that while these plans are laid out in the spirit world, many people are unaware of them because the flesh weighs more heavily on the spirit, like an airplane that has difficulty taking off and flying but has wings and an engine. And you here on earth are asleep and not being interactive in what would be beneficial to you. That's where my heart hurts; it's been particularly because of this that I've been staying long hours teaching the word of God because I want God to open the eyes of believers to see. Did you know this? Things are being planned now in the heavenly places. For example, the accidents happening on the roads and highways now are not necessarily natural or normal accidents; they are the results of the demons' activities.

One can be active and awake while watching a movie or a soap opera or when reading a newspaper or a novel. However, when it's time to follow the teaching of God's Word or to read a Christian book or the Holy Bible, one immediately begins to snooze and, consequently, fall asleep before finishing. You may even begin to develop laziness and go into procrastination, that is, postpone the time of prayer, of studying the Word, or going to church with other brothers and hearing the Word of God. There are even those who fall asleep in church when the Word is being preached or taught. Many times, this sleep is caused by the devil in the spiritual arena because he blows over the person's eyes, weakening and discouraging him. It creates a detour from the main focus that is the edification of his spiritual life and the strengthening of his communion with God.

There are sleep demons. At the party, the person doesn't sleep, but at church or following a sermon on TV, the dream weighs heavy on his eyes. Why all this? Because the devil doesn't want to see man's progress. He tries to keep him away from God, attacking everything that comes from God.

To prove to you that this kind of sleepiness and discouragement comes from the devil when it comes to hearing or studying the Word of God, I present to you the case of Eutychus. This is how Luke narrates it in the book of Acts of the Apostles, 20:7-9 NIV, "On the first day of the week we came together to break bread. Paul spoke to the people and kept on talking until midnight because he intended to leave the next day. There were many lamps in the upstairs room where we were meeting. Seated in a window was a young man named Eutychus, who was sinking into a deep sleep as Paul talked on and on. When he was sound asleep, he fell to the ground from the third story and was picked up dead."

This young man attended a service where Paul was preaching, and the service that day took longer than the other days until a deep sleep came over him, and he fell and died. Did God want Eutychus to die? No, but remember that the devil comes to steal, kill, and destroy (John 10:10). He attacks when we give him an opportunity. That is why the Scripture exhorts, "Neither give place to the devil"

(Ephesians 4:27 NIV). So, of course, Paul came down, prayed for the young man, and he was resurrected. But he had died during service because of sleep - he took a nap at the service. There's an old motto that says, "if you snooze, you lose." So don't sleep in your spirit. Wake up, and Christ will shine on you!

There is Heaven, where God has placed his throne, but there are heavenly regions or places. For example, God transcends beyond the limits of time, space, and matter. This is why God is Spirit (John 4:24). He is not controlled or confined by the physical world, for He does not die, does not age, and time does not control Him. God lives outside of time, but he controls time. He created time so that He could redeem man, for the Lord has always lived in eternity. Now, we here on earth, as human beings, are often influenced by time. So, at some point, one begins to age, have vision problems, have gray hair, walk with a cane, and have wrinkles on the face. What happens here? Simple, time works on man's organism (body), making him realize that this physical body is finite, fragile, and has a certain time on earth. All this because of Adam's sin - the first man, created in the image and likeness of God who sinned and fell from the dominion given by God.

It's easy to evaluate time. For instance, when you were two years old, you were not what you are now; time has changed you until now, transforming you.

CHAPTER XI

Understanding demonology

In the book of Genesis 6:1, we read, "And it came to pass when men began to multiply on the face of the earth...". Who multiplied? Men. Okay, take note of this because it's a key point in understanding what we are going to learn next.

To recap and, continuing in the same chapter, we read, "And it came to pass when men began to multiply on the face of the earth, and daughters were born unto them, That the sons of God saw the daughters of men that they were fair; and they took them wives of all which they chose. And the Lord said, My spirit shall not always strive with man, for that he also is flesh: yet his days shall be an hundred and twenty years. There were giants in the earth in those days; and also after that, when the sons of God came in unto the daughters of men, and they bare children to them, the same became mighty men which were of old, men of renown. And God saw that the wickedness of man was great in the earth and that every imagination of the thoughts of his heart was only evil continually" (Genesis 6:2-5 KJV). That said, and given the cruelty, violence, and wickedness on the earth, God instructed Noah to build an ark.

When God created the Heavens and earth, notice that in Genesis 1:1 (NIV), it doesn't say that in the beginning, God created the "Heavens" - in the singular. There is no reference to God creating Heaven, but the text says, "In the beginning, God created the Heavens and the earth." I would like you to follow me very closely here. In the beginning, God created "the Heavens," not "the Heaven," for Heaven already existed because that is where God dwells. "In the beginning, God created the heavens and the earth."

The expression "the heavens" means "heavenly places." So, what did God put in the heavens? The Angels.

Angels were originally created spiritually, and they were not meant to have physical bodies like humans. They had angelic status from the beginning to the end. God created them to be angels, or simply "ministering spirits," that is, servants. That was the angels' job: to serve God and men. For whatever God wanted to do here on earth, He could send the angels to do it, and they are the same angels who serve Him in Heaven as well.

Now, in the Genesis text that we have just read, Moses uses the expression "sons of God" in contrast to "sons of men."

In this text, we see that the sons of men were multiplying on earth, and girls were being born to them, human women here on earth. However, some of the angels were in the heavens. What are the heavens here? Heavenly places. These angels began to enjoy the daughters of men here on earth to marry them and have children. Remember, angels have wills, make moral choices, and are by nature highly intelligent. They can choose to rebel against God or to obey him. If they didn't have this free will, God wouldn't have allowed angels to sin against Him but would have sovereignly prevented them.

Some of these angels looked at the women here on earth and decided to become incarnate, that is, have human bodies, to marry them. Again, note this, as it is very important: angels (not demons) were converted to marry women (daughters of men). They left their dwelling place. Then, those angels married the daughters of men, and those daughters became pregnant, and the first human hybridism arose: the mixing of heavenly beings with human beings.

Consequently, the children born from that union between fallen angelic beings and (human) women were not normal human beings, like Noah. They were hybrids. Soon, there was a modification in man's genetics; he no longer had Adam's genetics, but the devil's genetics: a mix of part angelical and part human, causing a transformation in man's chromosomes and original nature.

And these children were not normal. They grew to a greater height than normal humans: they were the first giants to exist on the face of the earth. They were very evil and began to afflict normal humans like us, even to the point of becoming cannibals. The Adamic race was contaminated by the race produced by the fallen angels.

So, children were born who were not normal, and suddenly, the earth was filled with violence and evil. The heart of man became completely corrupted, and aversion against goodness was the dish of the day. What happened next? God decided in Heaven, "I am going to eliminate men on earth because if I don't do this, those who will live on earth will not be sons of Adam, but sons of the serpent, that is, sons of the devil."

Even now, some people are of the generation of the serpent, which is not normal human beings like us. They are among us; they were even born in the country where you were born, and if by coincidence you marry one of these people, you are marrying a demon. These people cannot be converted, no matter what apostle, prophet, pastor, or evangelist preaches to them. They can change churches; they don't change. They are children of the serpent. It's a generation mixed with ours, but they are not ours, although they also have a physical body. You walk into a street, a supermarket, a school, or a workplace, and some are there. They have a skin coating like us, but inside, they are whitewashed graveyards - corrupted and full of all kinds of venom and evil. They distill the poison from their mouths and take pleasure in the destruction and annihilation of human beings, descendants of Adam. It's easy to understand this if you are a personal [natural] man or woman.

Jesus used several parables to try to teach this to his first disciples and the people who followed him, but many didn't understand.

For instance, the parable of the wheat and the tares. Who is the wheat? The sons of the kingdom, and who are the tares? The children of darkness, children of the serpent. Notice that the wheat and the tares are so similar that the field owner had to tell the farmers, "Leave them until the harvest." Because in attempting to remove the tares, they were in danger of removing the wheat as well. He even stated, "an enemy sowed this when you were asleep at night." Satan has sown the heavens and made them so much like us that the angels will have work to do when Christ returns, to separate some to eternal life in the heavenly Jerusalem, and others to eternal punishment, in the lake of fire.

The parable of the net typifies and vindicates the same situation in which humanity finds itself. The net is cast and catches all kinds of fish. But taken to the ground, men choose the good fish and throw away the bad ones. The fish here refers to good fish, children of the kingdom, and bad fish, children of darkness. In the explanation Jesus gave, he made it understood that on the last day, the holy Angels would separate some for salvation and others for eternal punishment, where there will be weeping and gnashing of teeth.

Let no one fool you; we are not all normal human beings living on the face of the earth. Some beings are not people. Why do you think there is so much violence on earth? Endless wars, exacerbated hatred, and envy? The children of the devil are among us, facilitating the work of their father, Satan. They are bloodthirsty people, without pity for human life. Their ambition for power and their greed for money and fame deceive them and serve as the fuel that moves them to lie, kill, and steal. Even if people died in mass or thousands, it doesn't matter to them; it pleases them because they never had any love for humanity. Even in Jesus' time, these types already existed.

For example, in John 8:44 (NIV), Jesus said, "You belong to your father, the devil, and you want to carry out your father's desires. He was a murderer from the beginning, not holding to the truth, for there is no truth in him. When he lies, he speaks his native language, for he is a liar and the father of lies." Thus, Jesus faced those who even camouflaged themselves behind religion.

Nowadays, you find them in almost every environment: religious, political, economic agents, in sports, among others. It's another seed alongside the seed of God. One thing is common to them: they resist the truth, reject the light of God, and fight against goodness. They have no love for their neighbor because they have no God. Therefore, they can never be saved. Hence, God has prepared an eternal fire for the devil and his angels, and they will go with them.

If the waters of the flood consumed Noah's first world, this one is waiting for fire and brimstone. Thus, the Scripture testifies, "But they deliberately forget that long ago by God's word the heavens came into being and the earth was formed out of water and by water. By these waters also the world of that time was deluged and destroyed. By the same word, the present heavens and earth are reserved for fire, being kept for the day of judgment and destruction of the ungodly" (2 Peter 3:5-7 NIV).

Dear reader, you must know this because you don't know who you are sitting with, married, or dealing with. Therefore, you must be prudent and have spiritual discernment. There is another generation in our midst that is not normal. Those can hear the Word of God from morning until night, and they won't change. They can change churches a thousand times; they won't change at all. They are another generation in our midst; they are the generation of the serpent, the devil, and children of darkness, reserved for eternal fire.

That is why I advise young people to pray and ask for God's revelation before getting married.

The question of character is essential. Jesus called them "Brood of vipers." Notice the text in Matthew 12:34 (NIV) "Brood of vipers, how can you who are evil say anything good? For the mouth speaks what the heart is full of."

John the Baptist, Jesus' forerunner, had also already made mention of this word, and the text of Matthew 3:7 (NIV) vindicates it, "But when he saw many of the Pharisees and Sadducees coming to where he was baptizing, he said to them: "You brood of vipers! Who warned you to flee from the coming wrath?"

Now, the word brood in this context means character, generation, or species. The viper represents Satan, the ancient serpent, who deceives human beings Therefore, the Holy Spirit imprinted in my heart that I write this book to open humanity's eyes to the reality of the spiritual world. These are not human children; on the contrary, they are a generation infiltrated here on earth, causing malice to human beings. They are incorrigible and irreconcilable. Satan possesses them as his agents in a human body. This is why wickedness on earth tends to grow.

It's not a coincidence that some of you were doing well in life until you got into a relationship with certain people, and life became stagnant and blocked to this day.

Many of you can see that some of these people don't miss church or pick up the Holy Bible to be led to think that they are from God when, in fact, they are not. They may even preach, talk about God, but they are not! They will oppose everything that is of God, everything that is God's plan here on earth; they will resist. It's another seed that the devil has put into their body through those evil spirits.

In 2 Corinthians 11:14-15 (NIV), the Holy Scripture says, "And no wonder, for Satan himself masquerades as an angel of light. It is not surprising, then, if his servants also masquerade as servants of righteousness. Their end will be what their actions deserve." Just as God has his ministers and messengers, Satan also has his. And if the people of God don't pray and have discernment, many may be deceived into worshiping Satan, thinking that he is God. Not surprisingly, the culmination of all this will be the rise of the antichrist.

Back to the children - the fruits of miscegenation between angels and human women. So, these giants were born and grew up. God then had Noah make the ark with which he would judge the first world, with the flood, as we read previously. This world we are in now is the second world, not the first.

Why did God destroy the first world with the waters of the flood? Because of these abnormal creatures. When God sent the flood, there were only eight people then; only eight people were not corrupted: Noah, his wife, his three sons Shem, Ham, and Japheth, and his three daughters-in-law. These were saved.

Often, we tend to teach that Noah preached to people to get on the ark, and they wouldn't. But a thorough study of the Scripture shows otherwise. God told him to make the ark for him and his family because the world was corrupted.

The text in Genesis 6:11 describes the earth as follows, "Now the earth was corrupt in God's sight and was full of violence... So make yourself [Noah] an ark of cypress wood; make rooms in it and coat it with pitch inside and out " (Genesis 6:14 NIV). Furthermore, verse 21 says, " You are to take every kind of food that is to be eaten and store it away as food for you and for them." The expression "them" here referred to the animals and birds he was to take into the ark two by two. Noah preached to the humans to repent, but they refused and consequently didn't enter the ark. Noah was six hundred years old when the flood of waters came over the earth. Noah, his sons, his wife, and his sons' wives went in with him into the ark because of the flood's waters. Of the clean beasts and of the beasts that are not clean, and of the birds and every creeping thing upon the earth, they went in two and two to Noah into the ark, male and female, as God had commanded.

One must understand that it wasn't Noah who closed the ark door so that unrepentant people wouldn't enter, but God. So, the Scripture testifies, "...then the LORD shut him in" (Genesis 7:16). Why did God shut the door? To preserve the Adamic human race that hadn't allowed itself to be corrupted and retained Adam's original DNA. In this case, Noah and his nuclear family feared God and was an upright, righteous, and honest man.

Chapter XII

Enlightening questions

Now, three questions need to be answered for the understanding of demonology:

First question:

When the water came, what happened to those women who had married those angels? Well, they died, drowned in the waters of the flood.

Second question:

Those angels who had married the women (daughters of men), did they die too?

The answer is farsighted: No, because they couldn't die. Remember that they were spirits! Jude 1:6 (NIV) says, "And the angels who did not keep their positions of authority but abandoned their proper dwelling—these he has kept in darkness, bound with everlasting chains for judgment on the great Day." The New King James Version reads, "And the angels who did not keep their proper domain, but left their own abode, He has reserved in everlasting chains under darkness for the judgment of the great day." They remained alive here on earth and became demons. We can see here the governmental authority and holiness of angels. Angels were responsible for garrisoning or administering a territory. It's like having a government that sends soldiers to protect the population in a specific locality. Part of the soldiers fall in love and marry women from that region and get them pregnant when they should just be doing their patriotic duty. When this is the case, this is called abuse of authority, and they are penalized and can be arrested and held in military barracks or military prisons. This is almost what happened to these angels who failed to honor their status.

Third question:

What happened to the children born from the union between fallen angels and women (daughters of men)? Did they die too?

Here is where I want to give you a compelling part, a revelation: The answer is no. The spirits of these children of angels were transformed into what are now called evil spirits or familiar spirits. There is an important aspect to note, which characterizes these spirits: they have a thirst and anxiety to occupy human bodies and live in them. Do you know why? Because they can't go back to Heaven because they didn't come from Heaven, they were born on earth; that's why they seek to possess human beings at all costs; they want to enter them and live off the mental and vital energies of these possessed human beings.

In contrast to these evil spirits or demons, the fallen angels are not obsessed with possessing human bodies because previously, they had no human bodies. By the way, these are chained in eternal prisons. However, parallel to them, there are also rebellious angels: those who accompanied "Lucifer" and now Satan, when he was cast out. These are not imprisoned. The book of Revelation 12:7-9 describes this angelic company that Satan has also called "The Devil." Thus, it says, "Then there was a war in Heaven. Michael and his angels fought against the dragon, and the dragon and his angels fought back. But the dragon was not strong enough, and he and his angels lost their place in Heaven. The giant dragon was thrown down out of Heaven. (He is that old snake called the devil or Satan, who tricks the whole world.) The dragon with his angels was thrown down to the earth." These Scriptures make it abundantly clear that Satan has angels cast down with him from Heaven to Earth and the sea. They are furious because they know that their days of being cast into the lake of fire are approaching. As verse 12 of the same chapter attests, "So rejoice, you heavens and all who live there! But it will be terrible for the earth and the sea because the devil has come down to you! He is filled with anger because he knows he does not have much time."

There are three categories of devil angels

First: those who were hasty with Satan, also called the third

Second: those who have corrupted themselves with human women

Third: the demons, part of which are the fruit of the close union between fallen angels and women (the serpent's seeds). It's important to note that they don't operate in the same way, but they are all subservient to the devil - they are his vassals and operational agents on earth, fighting against God's plans and humanity. The hasty angels with Lucifer and the demons are working right now, as others are chained in eternal prisons.

Now, the devil's angels are different from the demons, although they all have the same master to whom they are accountable and from whom they receive instructions. These evil angels are not concerned with possessing the human body, although, on some occasions, they do. However, they are not thirsty to possess the human body because they didn't have it initially. These are the ones who are subdivided into the princes of darkness, principalities, powers, and spiritual hosts of wickedness, according to Paul's description in Ephesians 6:12.

I didn't put them in the order in which Paul placed them because, in his hierarchy, that is not the linear order. He only put them that way for exposition and exhortation to the brothers in Ephesus. These are territorial spirits concerned with controlling territories, countries, nations, states, provinces, and cities, among other regions of greater population agglomeration.

Now, demons, also called unclean spirits or foul spirits, have no choice but to find lodging in someone's body, so they will do everything they can to enter a person and make their life hell.

God had promised the salvation of humanity through the seed of the woman, and the woman would crush the head of the serpent, according to the book of Genesis 3:15. However, Satan thought he would corrupt and compromise God's plan when the fallen angels married human women looking for the one who could be God's chosen one to corrupt his seed. But he failed remarkably. Later, we read about

Mary conceiving the Spirit, giving birth to the child, and naming him Jesus.

This explanation is fundamental. Remember that in Genesis 3, Satan already existed, but in spiritual form. Therefore, to be legal and functional on earth, he sought a physical expression by entering the serpent that tempted Eve. As a result, he led her husband astray, thus breaking the communion between Adam and God. In chapter 6, which we read earlier, we find these other angels wanting to marry women.

Note that the devil doesn't make new demons: they are the same spirits here on earth thousands of years ago because the devil is not a creator but a creature, inferior to God in everything. What happens is that the spirits are more powerful and stronger in relation to human beings. Hence why the devil's Kingdom was installed on earth very quickly. For this, Jesus had to come here on earth to bring us the Kingdom of Heaven to destroy the kingdom of darkness to which men are subjugated. John states, "For this purpose, the Son of God was manifested, that he might destroy the works of the devil" (1 John 3:8 KJV).

As I mentioned in the previous lines, most fallen angels act as territorial spirits: they occupy territories, they occupy countries, districts, nations.

The following are some examples for further clarification on this matter.

Example 1: Who of you has ever been in a country, but whenever you travel and leave, it feels better away than when you are in it? It has happened to me several times. For example, once in the past, when I went to Swaziland, Kingdom of Eswatini, or South Africa, I felt different from when I'm in Mozambique. Why does this happen? Because in each country, there are devil angels, principalities, and powers that occupy areas of their territorial jurisdiction, whose actions vary from place to place.

Example 2: If the principality and demons that make its influence heavy are of drunkenness in an area, people living in that area will be inclined to consume alcohol, affecting all walks of life from underage children to the elderly. And if it's a principality or prostitution demons, people will be inclined to a sensual, lustful bohemian life. Finally, if the principality and demons are of drugs, the community or society will face high consumption of drugs and narcotics.

If you are spiritual and sensitive, you will see that this is a general problem covering a community or society. It may even be a provincial, state, or national issue, typical of a region controlled by a certain kind of power. Why? Because it depends on the individual forces that control that place. Now, these powers and principalities don't go alone; when they discover a territory and take control over it, they call demons to possess the people. So, it's possible to find a legion in a person. I will explain that in a moment.

For now, understand that the powers don't seek to possess your human body; it's those demons - unclean spirits devoid of a physical body, who seek to occupy people's bodies. In turn, the powers have the mission of arranging new bodies and opening the doors for the unclean spirits to enter. Each demon represents a problem, and when they possess a person, that person starts to have the same issues that the devil represents and manifests a behavioral picture typical of that demon. The demon finds physical expression visible through the person he possesses.

So, when Jesus Christ met with that madman of Gadara in Mark 5, it was one spirit who spoke singularly on behalf of the others as their spokesman. They were a legion. Legion is a military term used by the Roman army to describe an army consisting of two to three thousand soldiers. So, this man from Gadara must have had almost three thousand demons living in him, making him mad and giving him the strength to break chains and shackles. He was indomitable, and no one could bind him. Jesus asked, "What is your name?" Surprisingly, the two thousand or three thousand demons didn't speak; only one spoke. He said, "My name is Legion, for we are many." Why didn't he say, "We are legion"? Why did he speak in the first person, "My name is Legion, for we are many"? Because this was a power and not a mere demon without power in the spiritual rank. It's easy to distinguish this one from the rest of the demons because he asked Jesus to send them to the pigs, "Send us among the pigs; allow us to go into them." He could leave the individual, but not the area. So, this spirit was an angel of darkness - a power that owned and controlled that whole region.

He discovered this unoccupied house called "human being" and invited the lower fellows to come and live in it when he first occupied it. Finally, however, he became the house owner as one who has the title and a certificate of improvements to that building called "human being or person."

To demons, the human being is seen as a house - a residence. They are desperate to possess a body and don't feel good when there is no one to possess because they need human bodies and mental energies.

I pray that God will help you understand what I am explaining to you. May He open your eyes so that you can see.

Chapter XIII

Organizational structure and the diabolic operations

How do the operations of the dark angels take place?

Notice once again the text in Ephesians 6:10-12 (NIV), "Finally, be strong in the Lord and in his mighty power. Put on the full armor of God so that you can take your stand against the devil's schemes. For our struggle is not against flesh and blood, but against the rulers, against the authorities, against the powers of this dark world and against the spiritual forces of evil in the heavenly realms."

When Paul says, "For we do not have to fight against flesh and blood," in allusion to human beings, where do they come in here? Well, it's because the spirits we have to fight against, including demons, don't have flesh and blood, and we are not to fight them using human or physical weapons. Our fight is not against human beings but against principalities, powers, the princes of the darkness of this century, the spiritual hosts of wickedness.

From where do all these forces of darkness operate? From the principalities, the powers, the princes of the darkness of this world, and the spiritual hosts of wickedness? From the heavenly places. It's in the heavenly places where they move and plan their attacks on men.

I repeat these here are called territorial powers or spirits, as they seek to control territories. Although defeated, the devil is very organized in his organizational and operational structure. Note that Satan is one, not two. God is omnipresent; Satan cannot be omnipresent because he is a creature; he is a kid, concerning the LORD, our God. But how can he manage to harm people in Africa, Asia, America, and Europe at the same time if he is one? How is he able to do all of this evil management?

The answer is that he has a well-organized structure, a well-structured kingdom, and is not divided; all his agents are very united. The characterization of the organization and the organized structure leads us to take this matter very seriously. Satan is our adversary, and we must be armed with the knowledge of his operations so that we can stop his attacks and destroy his arsenal.

The powers are so tightly knit that even if a person travels from one country to another, the power that controls the country from which the person left will communicate to another power that controls that new country, saying, "Here comes someone, he is surrendered to your jurisdiction." And when the person enters that territory, the demons that were troubling him in the country he left may even stop at the border and not enter the new one. Thus, the person is handed over to other principalities and demons in the new country where the individual will live; and this ensures the continuation of the torments. There is cooperation among spirits, and there are also good offices with the demons of that country to torment the person, continuing the human expedient.

This is why even if people leave their land for another land far away, the escape will only be physical. Still, the spiritual connections prevail, and their effects continue to produce the impact. This organization and structure lead people to suicide, seeing no way out of their problems because there is no place or land where they can take refuge and be sheltered from the evil influences that chain and imprison them. Spirits have control over humans who ignore their *modi operandi*.

(This explains what you see in the videos of my apostolic missions abroad, people of African or other origins are persecuted even in Europe by spirits from Africa or from a past that took place far from where they are today).

That's why there are people who flee from one country to another, thinking that life will be better, and even there, things get worse. If someone can't get married in Mozambique, even if he leaves here for France, South Africa, or Australia, he may remain single because that power and demon won't leave him alone. So, if one goes, there will be a spiritual migratory process. That is why, from suffering so much and seeking answers without success, many commit suicide.

There at the border, as the person stamps his physical passport, the spirits communicate, "There he is, he's coming in. So, employ others who are on that side to continue with the work because he has already left our jurisdiction." Do you see? They have a map and spiritual G.P.S.; they know how to detect, "He has just left Mozambique, he is now entering Portugal, Brazil, please take care of him there." This way, other evil spirits are employed to continue the work that those in Mozambique stopped doing. There is demonic spiritual diplomacy going on in the spiritual arena daily. But human beings are not aware of it.

This is why, even if you move from one country to another, you may still have the same problems you had before, worse or lessened. If you were unlucky in a given country and you think you will be lucky when you move to another country, you may still be unlucky there. The problem is in the country and the kind of powers and demons that control that person's life.

Many people think that the devil is disorganized and randomly launches his arrows, but the spiritual reality is quite different. The devil is super-organized and has a unified chain of command: he gives daily instructions to his spiritual agents.

If there is a problem in a home, and the woman decides to leave to go and join another man, if a demon has proved this problem, this woman will always be with her bundles on her head because, with that new person, the evil spirit will always have influence. The separations will not cease until there is liberation and impartation of the Holy Spirit and total surrender to God, combined with a life of prayer and intercession. This situation is also valid for men.

Dear reader, in the face of a spiritual battle, don't give up - perseverance to eternal life helps - only the persevering will have and see the glory of God!

Jesus said to the Samaritan woman, "You are right when you say you have no husband. The fact is, you have had five husbands, and the man you now have is not your husband. What you have just said is quite true" (John 4:17-18 NIV). Thus, Jesus broke the curse that was hanging over her life so she could get married and have no more problems. It's easy to understand this, considering that she believed in Jesus and, because of her testimony, many of the Samaritans also believed in the Lord Jesus as the Christ.

Sometimes a man may think that the problem is with his wife and decide to leave her. He leaves her and finds another of a different face, stature, status, and color, but, unfortunately, the cycle of successive separations continues.

I wonder what's behind this. He keeps getting divorced; the problem is not with the women he has had, but probably with himself, so this person needs deliverance; he needs Christ.

For example, someone can open a company, and it goes bankrupt. He opens a second one, a third one, and the same thing happens. Then, the person decides to leave this place to another, and the same episodes occur. What is happening? The problem is not with the territory; it's with the person. Hence why when you are blessed in life, no matter where you go, you will continue to be blessed.

This is why Paul said, "Praise be to the God and Father of our Lord Jesus Christ, who has blessed us in the heavenly realms with every spiritual blessing in Christ" (Ephesians 1:3 NIV). In other words, if you are blessed in heavenly places, it doesn't matter whether you go to America, Africa, Europe, or Asia: you are blessed- blessed not to be cursed.

Dear reader, be aware of how organized and well-structured the devil is in his actions and performances. He is tireless, cunning, and at the slightest distraction, he takes possession of anyone, and from then on, he will dance to his tune, his way, and his pleasure. Therefore, pray for God to open your eyes to see and discern. May God grant you the intelligence and wisdom to take a right and discerning attitude.

Jesus said, "Come to me, all you who are weary and burdened, and I will give you rest" (Matthew 11:28 NIV). So cast off all your burdens, give up the old things, and give way to your savior. Breakthrough your limitations and enter into the fullness of grace. Then, dear reader, you can pray, declaring the words of Isaiah 50:4 "The Sovereign Lord has given me a well-instructed tongue, to know the word that sustains the weary. He wakens me morning by morning, wakens my ear to listen like one being instructed." "I am free from all covenants and curses, in the name of Jesus. Thank you, Father."

CHAPTER XIV

Two Success Factors

God said to Abraham, "Look around from where you are, to the north and south, to the east and west. All the land that you see I will give to you and your offspring forever " (Genesis 13:14-15 NIV). No matter where Abraham went, he was blessed. All he needed was to "look around from where he was." It is essential and urgent to distinguish two success factors here:

First: The place you are at and from which you project your vision.

God said to Abraham, "Look around from where you are to the north and south, to the east and west." Someone may think of a merely physical place, but that is not how to interpret spiritual things. Remember, Abraham was a man of faith, and to this day, he is called the Father of faith. He didn't need to arrange a ladder, scaffolding, or climb a tree from which he could project his vision. He looked with the eyes of faith. Abraham was in a superior place - he was with God and in God. He was in a position of advantage. You, too, as a son or daughter of God in Christ, are in a place of advantage, for it's a higher region than this world. Therefore, you must develop an awareness of where you are in Christ.

Second: Your vision counts: amplify it.

God said to Abraham, "Look around...." What do you see? You must write down the vision and make it very clear on tablets for yourself and for those whom God sends to help you. No matter your current condition or the adverse circumstances that manifest themselves around you: look at life with the eyes of faith, eyes of the spirit, and you will see no barriers or limitations because you are in Christ. Don't look down, but up. David said: "I lift up my eyes to the mountains — where does my help come from? My help comes from the Lord, the Maker of heaven and earth" (Psalm 121:1-2 NIV).

In this day and age, you must realize that the meaning of this text has no relation to a physical hill because you may be living in a city or village where there are no hills. How then will you raise your eyes to the hills that don't exist? The mount of Zion at the time represented a place of encounter with God, from where help and provision were given to the people of God when they prayed and sought him in these physical places. However, Jesus came to clarify for us that God is Spirit and is not confined to a merely physical place. He can be worshiped anywhere by someone who has his spirit enlightened and a pure heart. "God is spirit, and his worshipers must worship in the Spirit and in truth" (John 4:23-24 NIV).

The time has come when the worship of God can be done anywhere, as long as you connect your spirit to the Spirit of God through the Word, tuning into the proper, heavenly frequency to see the news and glories of God and not the horrors of this world.

Therefore, we preach the gospel so that people will believe, be saved, and be born again through the regeneration of the Holy Spirit. Then, they will have their spiritual antenna sharpened to connect with God anywhere, anytime, and at any moment because God is Spirit, and so is man. Therefore, your physicality shouldn't be a barrier when it comes to communion with God or worship of Him. In the bedroom, in the living room, in the kitchen, on the mountain, in the office, in the temple, or in the desert: you can worship God. This is what Jesus wanted to explain to the Samaritan woman. Abraham had already understood this secret thousand of years ago. That is why he pitched his tents from place to place, always considering the promised land: Canaan. Similarly, for us too, who in recent times have suffered countless restrictions on worshipping in the usual physical places, we need to continually train our spirits to meet God and worship Him without any physical hindrance; while waiting for the coming of our Lord and Savior Jesus Christ and preparing for the rapture of the Church. Yes, having our eyes fixed on the heavenly Jerusalem and the new Heaven and new earth, where there will be no more unrighteousness or iniquity, no more sickness or death, no more weeping or mourning; we will be with the Lord forever.

Dear reader, if you have accepted Jesus as your Lord and Savior, you are in Christ - in heavenly places above the devil. We will deal with this matter in the next chapter. But for now, understand that wherever you go, you are blessed in the city or country. Why? Because your blessing is there in the spirit, and it's from that place where it's assured, and your faith in God's Word is your policy.

Furthermore, if you have secured the blessing there, you will be productive no matter what sector you are placed in. Even if the general manager, superiors, or boss doesn't like you and puts you in a lower place or position, you will be blessed even there. Oh, glory!

In Joseph's life, we can notice this, son of Jacob: hated and sold into slavery by his own blood brothers. At his father's house, he was blessed. Sold and taken as a slave to Egypt and bought by Potiphar from the Ishmaelites' hands as their domestic servants, servants, and physical property. God was with Joseph, and in everything he put his hands to, he prospered until Potiphar surrendered to the grace that flowed in this young Hebrew blessed by God. He promoted him, placing him as a steward, a manager of everything and everyone except his wife.

Even his mistress, Potiphar's wife, surrendered to this young man, falling in love with him, a slave, to the detriment of the master, her husband. She tried to seduce him, but Joseph, for fear of God, ran away from her. She falsely accused him of attempted rape and unjustly arrested him; he was taken to royal prison. And what did he do in jail? Prisoner. Once there, he was given command, management over the prison and the other prisoners because of the blessing. From the moment he set foot in the cell, the conditions in the jail changed, and the boss is amazed as if to say, "You are going to be a boss here. You came in here as a prisoner, but your job now is to be the manager of everything that happens in this place." So Joseph is in jail, and his new job now is to head the other inmates. God's blessing was with him: in his spirit. He was the fruit of a covenant of blessings made between his parents: Abraham, Isaac, and Jacob. He had inherited generational blessings from his predecessors who had walked with God faithfully and worshipped him throughout their journey on earth.

CHAPTER XV

Your blessing doesn't depend on a physical place: it's in your spirit

Understand that it's not the place that counts; it's not the physical place you are in, but the spiritual place you are in, in the heavenly places.

The Holy Scripture records that at last, Joseph was summoned by Pharaoh to his palace to go and interpret his dream. Joseph shaved himself, knowing in his spirit that the time to shine had come. You know, when blessing comes or when something big comes or is about to happen in your life, you will know it. How? From your spirit, for it's your receiving place of all of God's blessings, spiritual blessings transmitted from the His Spirit to the spirit of man. The victory bell is given in your heart, and you can already begin to celebrate victory even amid battles.

In Joseph's case, we can note that Pharaoh had ministers, governors, scholars, and priests. Don't forget that ancient Egypt was a part of the cradle of science and the arts. Egypt had one of the first civilizations that mankind ever experienced. Therefore, Pharaoh was armed with prepared men and women.

Now, Joseph didn't even put in a resume. He didn't campaign or "brush up" on anyone. The young man is still in jail, but Pharaoh says, "We won't have anyone like this; from today, you are prime minister."

The man comes out of jail, directly into the government of Egypt's destinies. There were ministers and people technically well-placed and qualified to hold or aspire to this kind of administrative and governmental position. But the aspirants expired, and Joseph assumed the post on the same day. That post was created just for Joseph because no Egyptian had ever held it before. Joseph became prime minister in a foreign country. And his former boss, Potiphar, immediately becomes his subordinate and depends on him for his ration. Glory to God, "Jesus Christ is the same yesterday and today and forever" (Hebrews 13:8). You can read the rest of this story about Joseph in the book of Genesis, chapter 39.

In restoration, God reverses the roles - the slave becomes the master, and the master becomes the slave. In Luke 1:46-49 (NIV), we find Mary's song, acknowledging God's grace. "My soul glorifies the Lord, and my spirit rejoices in God my Savior, for he has been mindful of the humble state of his servant. From now on, all generations will call me blessed, for the Mighty One has done great things for me — holy is his name." With this, Mary wants us to understand that this God, whom we serve, is not a fiction, the result of thoughts, philosophical speculations, but the God of our history, the God who walks with us because he has done great things for us.

Dear reader, you need this God, so you need to accept Jesus Christ as the Lord and Savior of your life. And, being in Christ, you are also in the heavenly places, above all principality and demons. So, in practice, you need to secure your position there - in the heavenly places. In the following few chapters, we will learn how to do this practically. That's why I, for instance, am blessed, you know?

- It doesn't really matter if I go to Europe, America, it's the same thing. So, you too, no matter what sector or department you are placed in, don't worry. It's not the sector that counts; it's you and what you carry inside. Know that you are a child of the King of kings and a citizen of the Kingdom of Heaven. Therefore, you are above the circumstances of this world.

Challenges turned into successful testimonies

Many men of God had their challenges throughout their lives, but they turned their challenges into glory and successful testimonies because they had been blessed and walked with God.

For example, there were several episodes in which King Saul wanted to kill David but couldn't. Saul threw his spear in one of them, saying, "I'll pin David to the wall." But David eluded him twice" (1 Samuel 18:11 NIV). He put David in charge of the army and sent them where the battle was most intense and bloody, with the strongest and fiercest enemies. He thought David would die. So says the Scripture in 1 Samuel 18:25 (NIV), "Saul replied, "Say to David, 'The king wants no other price for the bride than a hundred Philistine foreskins, to take revenge on his enemies.'" Saul planned to have David fall by the hands of the Philistines." He set a trap to kill David because he was afraid of him, knowing that the Lord God was with the young shepherd. Verse 27 says that David arose and departed with his men, and they smote from among the Philistines two hundred men. And David brought his foreskins and gave them all to the king, that he might be his son-in-law; and Saul gave him his daughter Michal as his wife.

David saw every battle as a table prepared before his adversaries, as if to say, "Thank you. Therefore, you prepare a table for me before my enemies; you anoint my head with oil, and my cup overflows." David enjoyed intense battles because he knew he would win - being convinced of his God's power, greatness, and faithfulness. Saul sits down with his men, thinking, "This time, the kid will die because the war is intense there." And David comes back. "What's David like?" - and the young warrior, with a smile, said, "I killed them all. Here are the foreskins." I mean, the bigger the problems were, the more he was put in the most dangerous places where death was imminent or in an unproductive sector. Then, when he got there, everything started to be productive.

Dear reader, in the place where death is inevitable, you bring life, victory, and the possibility of growth there. Where there is discouragement, you bring cheer; where there is death, you bring resurrection, and where there is stagnation, you bring progress and dynamism.

For instance, David had great power, the power of the Spirit, and inner strength. He didn't waver in the face of challenges because he was convinced of this power, of God's greatness and his faithfulness. It's this strength that made him triumph and dismantle the snares of King Saul, a force that undoes the traps and the demonic strategies - a silent, discreet, but natural and efficient strength. So, the greater the challenge, the better it is to promote and validate this power. It's a gradation; from challenge to challenge, man grows in grace and victory because when we seem to be weak, then we are strong in Christ - empowered by the power of the Holy Spirit working in us.

Dear reader, I declare and prophesy that no matter the sector or department you are placed in, even if you are the most unproductive employee in the company or state department. Things will change when you get there because you are a bearer of blessings and are spiritually seated in heavenly places.

From company to company, you are blessed, regardless of the odds of it going bankrupt; God always brings divine provision, Therefore, circumstances shouldn't scare you since you are in the spirit, in the place of glory. However, there is one thing about us, as children of God, that many brothers and sisters need to discover and know - we are more than conquerors. Hence, even if someone comes and throws a spell or a curse on me, I neither cry nor mourn. I know in whom I have believed, and I know who I am: a child of the Kingdom, a heavenly citizen.

Listen: no matter how many directors or bosses come and go from the company, your blessing will be unchanging. No matter how many financial crises blow the world, how many companies fall into insolvency and close down, or how many people go bankrupt: you are not going bankrupt; you are going strong. Likewise, in the same spirit of faith, you can say with David, "A thousand may fall at your side, ten thousand at your right hand, but it will not come near you...no harm will overtake you, no disaster will come near your tent" (Psalms 91:7,10 NIV).

Repeat after me, "I go to valence, my value increases. So, I don't get worried."

If you are taking a professional course and say there is no market for it, don't worry; the market will be created because of you when you finish the course. There are some things God does to accommodate the good of his children, of those who love him and believe in him.

Chapter XVI

Spiritual Battles at the Higher Regions

Understanding the organizational structure of the diabolic angels

"For we do not wrestle against flesh and blood..." (Ephesians 6:12 NKJV).

Now, you have to understand that we are at war, every day - spiritual warfare. Not against human beings. However, we fight from a position of advantage: we have the blood and victory of Christ on the cross of Calvary. Many are preoccupied with fighting against people. Some fight against their wives, wives fight against their husbands, and so on. The man disfigures his wife's face and no longer wants to take a picture with her; he no longer wants her by his side when he is the one who caused the problem. In turn, the wife, tired of her husband's abusive behavior, bottles him up, and consequently, he no longer has a leading voice in the home. Because of this, when the thunderstorm comes, no one defends her at home, and even when burglars break into the house and enter to steal, the man has no voice because he is bottled up. Bottling or putting someone in the bottle is a metaphor describing enchantment to condition someone, taking away their critical ability and authority. It's the act of reducing the man or woman to passive obedience to the person who bottled him or her.

The Holy Scripture urges us not to fight against people but against the evil spirits that use and manipulate people, setting them against each other. Thus, members of the same family begin to fight against each other, hating and avoiding unnecessarily.

Notice here, "For we wrestle not against flesh and blood, but against principalities, against powers..." My desire is for you to realize one thing here: the sacred text doesn't say, "we wrestle against demons." Demons are foot soldiers, and sometimes, they move and operate as castes in the kingdom of darkness. However, in this context, Paul began to give categories of these upper-echelon administrative layers than the demons in the realm of darkness. He said, "For we wrestle not against flesh and blood, but against principalities…".

The principalities

The word principality means "magistrate" and refers to the first in hierarchy. These are supramundane powers often in conflict with God and his people. So, these are angels from the devil's side who are first in rank. Those angels who were cast to earth with the devil, some of them are first in rank. They also have demons in their service. In addition, they have greater authority than the others who are under them. They are the principalities that report directly to the devil about what the underlings do.

Chapter XVII

The powers

Powers, in governmental terms, are spiritual governments. This one, in particular, is tasked with controlling territories and is not concerned with possessing human bodies. Their main job profile is to gain more territories. And when that happens, they invite the demons that come like bees in masses to enjoy the party under their hierarchical command. Do you understand what I said now? They are not concerned with possessing bodies, but with possessing what? Territories influence the political life and laws of certain countries, states, or municipalities under their spiritual jurisdiction. And by owning territories, they influence the way people think in a particular community and try to stop the progress of God's work. There are places, for instance, where people may find themselves battling a certain vice that just won't seem to end; it's a power controlling that place.

When I went to Brazil in January 2018 to conduct a crusade in Rio de Janeiro, I remember. I first went to São Paulo, going through the Guarulhos Airport, and then took a connecting flight to Rio de Janeiro. We arrived there late at night, at around twenty o'clock, and it was almost dark. As we landed in Rio de Janeiro, God began to show me the power that controlled that particular state of Rio de Janeiro; and it was a spirit of war, of death.

I remember that on the same day that we arrived there, we heard that the mayor or police commander of Rio de Janeiro (I don't remember exactly) had been killed by drug dealers. With my spiritual senses, I even felt in my spirit the smell of cocaine and gunpowder. I concluded that the state's government would have to work hard against organized crime, but it wouldn't solve that problem; only the church could help if it was given importance and pedestal. Therefore, the church had to pray intensely, and only after that should the government intervene. This would facilitate any action that the state government might undertake to remedy the situation - to fight crime.

This is why the government has to work in accord with the local churches and the Church in general because many of the problems are spiritual and cannot be fought only scientifically.

There are indispensable social intervention agents:

1.   **The government,**
2.   **The academy where science is produced and**
3.   **The men of God.**

Now, in the intervening order, it's the men of God who should come first, then the rulers and the academics who intervene with science and technology. Why men of God and the church? Because the real battles are planned, and their attacks launched from the spiritual world that eludes modern science. For instance, there is no human ultrasound machine or X-ray device capable of detecting the presence of a demon in a person's eyes or body, nor binoculars capable of detecting dark angels in a given region territorially populated by human beings. However, there is a power - an anointing on some people called by God, which can detect demons and remove them from some people and neutralize the plans and influences of the dark angels. After territorial spiritual cleansing or human deliverance, then governments and academia can successfully intervene.

Tell me, for example, what would you do to force someone to stop drinking or using drugs? Someone who has been addicted since his or her youth? What would you do to make someone quit smoking if the addiction has been ingrained in their blood for a long time? What would you do to someone who sells his or her body on the street?

And if someone is used to stealing, how do you help him or her to stop this unethical bad habit? First, you have to keep in mind that a spirit of kleptomania possesses people - an uncontrollable urge to commit theft. For these kinds of people, nothing guarantees that they will stop stealing because no matter what you give them, it will never be sufficient.

Have you never seen or heard about workers in some companies who still steal even when their boss decides to raise their salaries? What do you need to change? Will, decision, and spiritual liberation.

There was a time in schools, when it was said that the undisciplined (unruliest) students in class, had to be head of the class to calm the others down. The logic or justification was that once he was in control of all the commotion, as head of the class, he would say to his classmates, "Friends, the jokes are over, I'm in charge now, let's behave well."

In practical life, this doesn't work; you won't take the boss of thieves and put him as the chairman of the company's board of directors because by doing so, you will be enlarging his market. Consequently, he will steal more, defalcating the company to the point of bankruptcy and putting many families in misery.

The background here is that certain people have behaviors and habits that are difficult to change, not because of them but because of the demons that possess them. And you can't do anything humanly or scientifically to help them change, except by the anointing of God, by the power of the Holy Spirit, and the Word of God that shapes an individual's character. The Scripture says, "Do not conform to the pattern of this world, but be transformed by the renewing of your mind. Then you will be able to test and approve what God's will is—his good, pleasing and perfect will" (Romans 12:2 NIV). God's anointed Word has the potential to transform and shape a person's character and life completely.

Do you think that an aggressive man who beats his wife from morning till nightfall, until she passes out and only wakes up with ice water on her body, is going to change just because of the sponsors and their advice? If the sponsors come, he might even say, "You pressed charges and exposed our private life, didn't you? If I used to slap you ten times, now I raise it; ten more." So, this way of becoming recurrent until the woman gives up on the relationship and leaves to avoid her death. This has been one of the causes of many divorces: behavioral incompatibility and bad attitudes from man to woman and woman to man. Life is spiritual.

For example, a man who lies to his wife and sleeps away from home for consecutive nights and then says, "I'm coming home from work late, the workload is higher, and we are few in the department." Next, the wife finds out that her husband has other women, and yet she says he has changed, but in practice, he continues with the same behavior. Do you think you will change him by stalking him or tracking his cellphone? It won't, my sister because he might be under the influence of a demon. He will not change just because you control him or because you put a truecaller (phone call tracking system or application) on his cellphone. He will only change if you pray for him and rescue him from the clutches of the devil. The Scripture encourages, "Save others by snatching them from the fire; to others show mercy, mixed with fear—hating even the clothing stained by corrupted flesh" (Jude 23 NIV). First, of course, you have to see how serious the situation is and ask the Holy Spirit for advice. Although you cannot let yourself die, you can wisely preserve your physical and moral integrity while it's still early. God has answers for everything because life is spiritual. It's in this dimension where it is controlled.

Understand that demons are more scientific than we human beings; they are crafty. Hence why the Word exhorts us to stand upright, "against the wiles of the devil" (Ephesians 6:11 KJV).

What is a wile? It's a trap. And the expression "crafty snare" conveys the idea of a well-planned, meticulous, and subtle trap, one that catches the person unnoticed. This is why Paul says, "...in order that Satan might not outwit us. For we are not unaware of his schemes" (2 Corinthians 2:10,11 NIV). When the devil wants to trap someone and destroy his life, he sets a trap thoroughly and attractively without the person knowing. He will never come and say, "Hello, I'm the devil, man's enemy. I want to enter your body to possess you, ruin you, and then kill you." No, he even transfigures himself as an angel of light. He is an experienced hunter. It's no coincidence that the Scripture encourages, "Surely he will save you from the fowler's snare and the deadly pestilence. He will cover you with his feathers, and under his wings, you will find refuge; his faithfulness will be your shield and rampart. You will not fear the terror of night, nor the arrow that flies by day" (Psalm 91:3-5 NIV). If you are spiritual and sensitive to the voice of the Holy Spirit, you will be warned beforehand about danger zones, and you will escape.

Many people have encountered the devil, but they didn't know it was him. They didn't recognize him.

The devil, Satan, or Lucifer is very intelligent, cunning, and a strategist. He is endowed with enviable knowledge through which he manipulates and camouflages the truth, distorting it. The devil is a master of persuasive, seemingly sane communication. Only God's knowledge and power can stop him. For example, in the temptation of Jesus, after the baptism in the Jordan River, the devil tempted Jesus based on the Holy Scriptures, distorting them (Matthew chapter 4 & Luke chapter 4). That is why people don't recognize him and consequently fall into his snares. But Jesus said, "If you hold to my teaching, you are really my disciples. Then you will know the truth, and the truth will set you free" (John 8:31-32 NIV). Set free from what? From the traps laid by the devil, the deviant influences and alienation of his spirit from man by deception.

Dear reader, understand that the devil is not as ugly as you may see in caricatures and illustrations depicting him with horns, a tail, and a fork in his hand. You have to study God's Word and know it to be able to identify the devil in people, conversations, and everyday situations and neutralize him. He looks very beautiful because he can transfigure himself and appear in the form of a man or woman and even an animal. He can turn into a woman and become the most beautiful girl in the area, and men appreciate her and enter into pacts with him. He can turn into a charming young man, with a strong, muscular physique, with an athletic, slender body, and women can't resist the temptation, "What man is this?" It's the devil, my sister, it's the devil, watch out! The Scripture says, "Resist the devil, and he will flee from you" (James 4:7).

Do you know how to discover the devil, whether it is him or not? Through his eyes, through the words that emanate from his evil character. Look at his eyes: they will reveal who you are dealing with, whether it is the devil or not. The eyes are the window of height; they reflect the inside of someone hidden in the physical body. Also, if you are spiritual and look at them, you will know that this is the devil. What to do next? Get away from him or rebuke him, "Get away from me, Satan, get behind my path, in the name of Jesus."

There are women whose nature is not entirely human; they are the incarnation of aquatic or marine divinities. Some women are queens in the underwater or marine world. To enter into a pact with them is to open the door to persecution. It's to subject yourself to a turbulent life. Hence, the need for spiritual discernment before any act or marriage.

Did you know that there are men and women who, right now, have many children in the dark spirit world? It's a fact. Every time a woman sleeps with a demon in the form of a spirit husband, also called "husband of the night," she can become pregnant and even have children with him, in spirit. Oh, this is serious! I have prayed for several women in this condition and have documented their stories and the positive transformation their lives have had by the power of God. I cast out demons and have battled with these spirits throughout my ministry. Therefore, I speak from revelation and ministry experience from many years of research and experience.

The wife or husband of the night leads to frustration. A relationship is established between the man or woman with the evil spirit or husband of the night when the two cross paths in dreams, either day or night. And, upon awakening, one doesn't see the person with whom they had a relationship and physical traces - a sensation of having engaged in a sexual act and ejaculation that actually took place. But the question is, with whom did the person have sexual intimacy? This spirit stretches the veil over people preventing them from having a normal relationship with the person. Women and men end up conforming to this state, refusing any relationship with real beings (real husband or wife) because they are spiritually married to demons.

I have prayed for women who had many children in the spirit, but they never had any in their normal flesh life; they were barren. Sometimes the devil even claims, "she is my wife! I want my wife." Many times, these people are not even aware of this spiritual condition. Still, they can see that in their practical-material life, things are blocked, and nothing works out, especially in relationships. Some even dream of sleeping with men and wake up wet with a feeling of having had a sexual experience. The same happens with men; some dream of sleeping with women at night and wake up wet. I do counseling sessions and have prayed for these kinds of people throughout my ministry. This is a spiritual reality. If someone doesn't believe the explanation I'm giving, how can they then question the experiences of several women and men who have been set free from this kind of spiritual prison, and their testimonies are documented in videos, with their consent and permission? This world is spiritual, and it's more real than the physical world. You have to be in the spirit to understand spiritual language and spiritual realities.

I once prayed for a sister who had three children by a demon. There are times that the devil uses people to help him multiply evil spirits.

Some men have slept with spirit women and got demons pregnant, and they have children in the spirit world now. Generally, these men have a common symptom and characteristic: they don't stay with the women. When they marry, they get divorced quickly because they are already married and have children in the spirit, so they have to be set free.

However, in the spirit world, when a woman becomes pregnant, she won't give birth to a physical-human baby because the father of that baby is not a human being; he is spiritual - a demon. Consequently, demons, evil spirits, filthy, unclean spirits multiply.

I'm telling you what happens in the spiritual world: life and daily activities are parallel to the physical world, but everything is spirit. The devil's greatest trick consists in convincing people to think that he doesn't exist and that the spiritual world doesn't exist. Thus, he easily catches them in their ignorance. The Scripture testifies, "And even if our gospel is veiled, it is veiled to those who are perishing. The god of this age has blinded the minds of unbelievers so that they cannot see the light of the gospel that displays the glory of Christ, who is the image of God" (2 Corinthians 4:3-4 NIV). But, as God's Word is taught, the light shines in the hearts of those who hear it, believe it, and live by it.

I have prayed for several women, and a demon could say, "This one is mine; she has my wedding ring." However, looking at her physical finger, you can't see any wedding ring. Why does this happen? Because he is referring to a spiritual alliance. This is why I explained earlier that the spiritual world is a sphere of spiritual activities.

The powers occupy territories and employ evil spirits to work for them and the Kingdom of Darkness

It's possible to enter a neighborhood, a house, or a place and feel that the atmosphere is strange and heavy.

Have you ever gone for a job interview or taken an exam at school, read everything, but when you got to the exam room and started having your mind blocked, blurred, and forgot the material? In this situation, the person wants to proceed or pass but is not succeeding.

Do you know why this happens? It's because that place is spiritually controlled. But God gives us the grace to take over new territories. God told Joshua, "Every place that the sole of your foot shall tread upon, that have I given unto you, as I said unto Moses" (Joshua 1:3 KJV). So, receive grace to control territories now, in the name of Jesus.

Note this: You won't enjoy the blessing in a territory you have not yet conquered. Jesus knew this. Looking at His three and a half years of ministry, we can notice that He never went preaching outside the borders of Israel. And, before His death and resurrection, He did not send His disciples outside of Israel. Why? Because it was before he died on the cross, dethroned the devil, and conquered the nations of the world with his blood. Only after his resurrection did Jesus empower his disciples to go into the rest of the world. Consider his words, "Then Jesus came to them and said, "All authority in heaven and on earth has been given to me. Therefore go and make disciples of all nations, baptizing them in the name of the Father and of the Son and of the Holy Spirit" (Matthew 28:18-19 NIV). First, he had to conquer the whole world through his blood. Now, he has made us kings and priests and given us his authority to go and preach the gospel in the entire world and to every creature. He bought the field for us, and we walk and act in his authority. He has given us power of attorney to use his name against the spiritual hosts of darkness.

Dear reader, understand that each level of glory in your life will result from our conquered spiritual territories. To ascend to each level, it's necessary to carry out a spiritual battle to clear the space of demons and powers and principalities. After that, you begin to enjoy the glories and benefits of that new level. You may notice that the more you grow in glory and success, the greater challenges and unprecedented opposition you begin to experience. Why? Because you are forcing the withdrawal of a power to take your place and live well. And they don't want to leave because they live off the energies of those places. It's like snatching a plate out of a hungry person's hands; it can cause a fight. The same thing happens in the spirit. That's why the Scripture says to grow from glory to glory, and our righteousness is from faith to faith (2 Corinthians 4:18; Romans 1:17). Faith and glory must go hand in hand since for each level of glory attained, it takes faith to maintain it and faith and knowledge or revelation to rise to a new higher level of glory. Therefore, the righteous will live by faith. One must dethrone the powers that control the territory, even to run a good evangelistic campaign.

Chapter XVIII

Evangelism versus territorial spirits

I remember the first time I went to St. Thomas to preach in 2018. We had scheduled a salvation and miracles crusade in Yon Gato square at four o'clock in the afternoon (4 pm). Yon Gato square is situated between the prime minister's palace and a crowded local market having streets on either side.

I was with my wife in one of the guesthouse rooms we had rented for my team and me to stay at. The other team members had already organized the event, and, during the day, the place was bustling with people. We had rented a stage and set up sound and light systems: everything was ready for the beginning of the event, and the praise team was ready to start. I was in the room preparing and praying for the event. I always do this before going to minister in big and small events. Then, when it was exactly four o'clock, I looked towards the window of the second-floor bedroom where I was, from the seaside, and my spiritual eyes opened. Suddenly, I saw a gigantic black snake flying out of the sea (Atlantic Ocean) and spitting a lot of water out of its mouth over that Island. At that moment, very heavy rain began to fall, and everyone on the streets near Yon Gato Square and the market vendors fled at dusk to their homes.

One of the missionaries who was helping organize the event came and knocked on my bedroom door, saying, "Apostle, can we cancel/reschedule the event for another day? It's just that there are no more people outside and the rain is very heavy. We fear for the equipment and the poor participation of people." Since I understood the spirit world, and God had revealed to me what was happening, I knew what to do because I had seen the source of the attack. I told him, "Let's not delay, no. Get ahead and start with the service. If there are no people, I will preach into the air." Then, my wife and I prayed, neutralizing the evil plans, and at the same time, trapping the power that controlled that country. The Holy Spirit said to me, "The serpent you saw came because of you. It represents the power that controls this Island and it's angry because of you. But I have given you the grace and anointing to liberate territories and people. St. Thomas will be for Christ, for I have people I love in this country, and I haven't forgotten them, so I have sent you." Then I prayed, "You, power of darkness who controls this Island, I break your hold on this country and these people, in the name of Jesus Christ! Take your hands off God's people!"

After we prayed, I went to the stage in the square to minister. I looked paranoid because there was no one there except my team and the family of brother Adilson, who had hosted us in his guesthouse, a very humble and warm man, and his wife - a believer and woman of faith as well. Pastor Janifer and the worship team started singing praises and worship to the Almighty God. Then, the missionary announced my turn to go on stage, and I did. All I remember is that I closed my eyes and started singing the song that goes, "Hallelujah, hallelujah, hallelujah, hallelujah, Jesus Christ, Jesus Christ, Jesus Christ." We sang as it rained torrentially, wetting our clothes. I knew in my heart that this was a day of great spiritual battle for souls. I had to open the way and take that territory for Christ. You can feel it in your spirit. Well, moving on, I sang with my eyes closed while the praise team consisting of Pastor Janifer and a sister accompanying us, who did the choir, and our organist played.

I was determined and knew that victory was ours. As the praise went up, I sang and prayed in my spirit simultaneously. Suddenly, the rain stopped, and people, some out of curiosity and others brought by the Holy Spirit, began to come. When I opened my eyes, the place was full of people. It was a night of glory, of miracles, signs, and wonders. Many souls were saved, lives were transformed, and many were healed and freed from various ailments that tormented them. The next day was also glorious, and, at the end of the mission, I was invited by Santomense Television for an interview. They were all amazed by the power of God and the prophecies, as I called person by person and told them the root of their problems, and they confirmed and were set free. Since the island is not too big, many knew each other. When I mentioned one, the others clapped their hands in confirmation and admiration, "How does he know all this about us, being his first visit to this seemingly forgotten country?" It was the power of God. The news spread all over the island, and the name of Jesus was glorified. Many of those who hadn't come to the crusade watched the interview in the news, and the name of the Lord was proclaimed in that country.

Now, a minister of the gospel who doesn't understand the spirit world would have given up the mission, postponed the crusade and returned home without having accomplished the mission. This is because these spirits are stubborn and don't usually give up easily on their territories. Hence, the Lord Jesus told me that my crusades of salvation and miracles would be called "Heavenly Atmosphere" because He gave me the grace to purify the spiritual environment of territories. But to do so, people, and especially rulers, must recognize God's prophets and value Him.

CHAPTER XIX

Dealing with the powers

Power doesn't need to go into every woman in a given family, claiming that they belong to him. What does he do? He alone controls them all and introduces those demons in his service (under his jurisdiction) into each of them.

This is why someone can go to church; the pastor casts out that unclean spirit, and the person goes home and still has the same problem because the power hasn't been arrested or neutralized.

Have you never seen a family in which everyone has (suffers from) almost the same problem? Someone might think that many demons are possessing the members of that family when they don't. Remember that each demon is a problem. It represents a certain problem for which it's responsible. The example above could be one power controlling everyone: men and women in the same family. You can see that no one gets married in that family, from the grandfathers to the grandchildren. It's necessary to do a spiritual x- ray of that family to detect the root of the problem that ails it.

In other cases, the power can block a family's professional life, even making it so that no one works or owns a home. And, whoever tries to get out of this dungeon, either dies or loses a job, to go back to having no money and, consequently, to stop building their house.

The powers don't need to enter a body. They control the area, the territory.

It's common, for instance, that on the one hand, in a family, all the women have children, but are living at home with their parents, therefore, without a home. And on the other hand, all the men have wives and children, but no one has a home of their own; they are all still living at home with their parents.

Some men work and have a good salary but have no home of their own, nothing but a lack of autonomy, living only to spend their money in endless addictions. Sometimes, they may even want to do something and take steps towards building something, but they can't; they are stuck spiritually. Even a good woman may appear, coming from God, to marry this man and save him, and finally, thanks to her, the man regains his autonomy. There are also cases in which, even if God sends a woman to a man in this kind of situation when she starts talking about getting land/plot of land to build his house or to acquire property because of the man's spiritual embargo and blindness, he may even leave her, thinking that she is bothering him. He starts looking at that woman as if she is mean and annoying. He doesn't want to hear those ideas of leaving his parents' house because the devil has already blinded his mind, and he thinks it's normal to grow old sleeping in a room of his father's house, disputing it with his sons or brothers.

The man may think that being delivered from evil spirits is a form of alienation. This happens because the devil has blinded his mind and spirit. So, any idea that would lead him to regain his autonomy, freedom and the independence of his mind becomes an annoying idea, contrary to God's will which is righteous and good. When hosted in our minds, the evil spirits determine the direction of our lives, what is his becomes ours. Thus, erasing in us what is originally our beneficial roadmap to our lives.

How many women have you heard saying, "My God, the movie I'm living today is similar to the one I heard my mother tell that happened to her when I was still a child!"

Furthermore, it's also common to hear a man say, "the situation I'm going through today is almost the same as the one my father told me he lived through when I was still a child. What happened to my grandparents, to my parents, is happening to me now. And it feels like I'm not able to control and reverse it. It's beyond my capacity." This is a sign that there is a dark force trying to control this family's life, from generation to generation. These spirits don't die; they survive the generations of a family, passing from person to person, changing the bodies they possess. Their end is the lake of fire, after the final judgment.

It's very common to see a man who has found a beautiful woman, but he says, 'I love you, you are beautiful, but I can't stay with you, I don't know why, but I can't." In all this, for you, a man coming from afar, you may look and be amazed, "Why is the other man leaving such a beautiful woman like that?" She is beautiful in others' eyes, but her husband's eyes see no beauty in her. All he sees is a demon, and everything is negative, so he mistreats her until they separate.

This is very serious! You need this information for your stability and happiness on earth. Knowledge sets you free.

I have seen men with beautiful women by sight. You know? - Beautiful, with everything a man can appreciate in a woman: hardworking, dedicated, humble, among other qualities, but every day her husband beats her. She cooks, and he doesn't eat. And he even says, "you are pretty, but I don't want you, go home to your parents." In this situation, it's either the man or the woman who is under a family power – they must seek help from God.

Now, for example, these kinds of powers, even if the person leaves the country to go and live abroad, it doesn't solve anything.

They will report to another power in that country to continue the foreign affairs in international diplomacy. So while the person stamps his passport at the border (at the migration services), they stamp the spiritual paper transfer passport.

In 2017, when I was in Porto, Portugal, some Mozambican sisters came and told me that they no longer wanted to return to Mozambique. I asked the reason, and they said that there were serious spiritual problems in their house and that every time they went to Mozambique to then return to Porto, they had marital problems. I told them that neither the country nor the neighborhood was really the problem, although in some cases, this happens. For instance, there are countries with a heavier and more disturbing demonic atmosphere than others, mainly in countries where the practice of witchcraft and sorcery is greater. In that case, you can even physically disconnect yourself from those places to seek new air. However, you will need the hand of God because spiritual problems are solved spiritually. So,

I prayed for those sisters, and they were set free. Today they are happy in their homes and have a stable professional life. In Christ, there is a solution to every kind of problem.

The same day that I prayed for these sisters, others were living in Germany who had gone to the crusade in Portugal, who said that even in Germany, they couldn't get jobs, nor get along with their (spouses) husbands. The men said that they couldn't get wives, even in Germany. So these evil spirits persecute them even in European countries.

I told them that it's not because of where they came from, but rather because of what was covering them spiritually. I prayed for them, and they were set free by the power of God. I met with some European brothers who told me they didn't want to go back to Europe because their professional life and business there weren't successful. I prayed for them too, and God has blessed their lives and businesses until today.

How to explain that in a family, almost all the women don't conceive? I mean, it seems that they all had the same path and have a certificate of infertility or sterility.

The reason I reveal this to you is because of what is happening in the spirit. But it's possible to reverse it completely by faith and prayer.

Never forget this: whoever gains dominion in the spiritual arena automatically controls the physical world.

Chapter XX

Princes of Darkness

"For we do not wrestle against flesh and blood, but against principalities, against powers, against the rulers of the darkness of this age, against spiritual hosts of wickedness in the heavenly places" (Ephesians 6:12 NKJV).

Princes represent high rulers in the hierarchy of the Kingdom of Darkness. They are first above all those we mentioned earlier. The word "prince" here doesn't mean "son of a King." These high- ranking evil spirits rule people through ignorance. They use ignorance to destroy them. Hence why they are called "princes of darkness." The expression "darkness" denotes ignorance, lack of knowledge. These spirits have the potential to block people's minds. It's these princes of darkness who often empower witches and wizards to work for the devil, fabricating and inflicting evil on people.

They don't want to see you study the Holy Bible, go to Church services, or pray. Why? Because they want to keep you in ignorance. They achieve their intentions at the expense of people's ignorance. Since it takes a deep understanding of how they operate and how to stop them, we will study them in more detail after I explain the spiritual hosts of wickedness.

CHAPTER XXI

Spiritual hosts of evil

"Against spiritual hosts of wickedness in the heavenly places."

The word hosts means "an army, a number, or a group of beings." So when you hear the word "hosts" in this context, it refers to a collection of evil spirits.

They usually act in a multifaceted way, together, inflicting evil and misery on human beings. These are the ones who have often barred the progress of many people's lives. If one discovers a house, he invites others to go there.

These spiritual hosts of wickedness are evil - highly evil. When they come into someone's life or a family, they leave no trace; they want to destroy everything. Furthermore, they don't want the good of anyone, and when they possess a person, they will want to do evil to other people and kill and destroy. They carry hatred and envy to men's hearts. They cause accidents and destruction, sowing grief and pain wherever they go.

Have you ever seen, for instance, people who only think of killing, fighting, destroying, or making others cry when they wake up in the morning? And they aren't satiated by the blood of those they have already killed; they have no sympathy for the weeping of those who have already shed tears - they are spirits of evil. They don't want friendship with you but your utter destruction. You don't see them, but they exist; you don't feel them, but they are out there. They act from heavenly places, controlling men on earth. These are the ones who often plan car or plane accidents and ships that are lost or shipwrecked at sea. Their purpose is to drink human blood. They are spirits of evil.

Dear reader, understand that day and night, evil plans are made in the spirit world to decimate, kill, annihilate, finish and destroy men here on earth.

It's the intercessions of the Church, the prayers of God's people that inhibit Lucifer and those powers from killing on earth, as they would have it. The prayers of the Church stop the advance of the Kingdom of Darkness and nullify the devil's evil plans in the spiritual arena. If we didn't pray, the world would probably be in unquenchable flames today.

These spirits work with the princes of darkness and can deceive as many people on earth as possible and on all continents. The princes of darkness would like to see the world population decrease - killing all human beings if it were up to them, but the believers' prayers stop them.

Throughout human history, the princes of darkness have used human figures and leaders to project macabre agendas against humanity, using deceptive pretexts, making lies the dish of the day. That's why they don't like churches, Christians; they don't like to see God glorified. Hence why, day and night, we have to intensify our prayers for humanity and for the kingdom of God. Jesus said, "And I also say to you that you are Peter, and on this rock, I will build My church, and the gates of Hades shall not prevail against it" (Matthew 16:18 NKJV)

Note well: I am singling out each of these spiritual agents of the devil singularly, for the sake of study and explanation, to make it easier for you, dear reader, to understand. First, however, you should know that they are all united when they are in operation because they obey a chain of command that comes from their leader: Satan – man's opponent.

CHAPTER XXII

Operations of the Princes of Darkness

In the book of Daniel 9, we find a scenario in which Daniel is praying. While he was praying, he decided to stay twenty-one days without eating or drinking anything, praying for Israel. From the books, he had read and understood that the number of years, of which the LORD spoke to the prophet Jeremiah, in which Jerusalem would be free from the colonial domination and yoke of Babylon was seventy years, as Daniel himself narrates (Daniel 9:2).

Note that there had been a prophecy from God through Jeremiah's mouth that God's people would be taken captive for seventy years, but they would be set free after that period. It turned out that although the time of freedom had come, according to the prophecy, God's people were still slaves. Had God lied, or was the prophet wrong? No. When a prophecy is given, it demands a corresponding action on its recipients' part, and this is connected with prayer. This is what Daniel did: he scheduled a twenty-one-day fast to pray and reinforce the fulfillment of the prophecy. Like a pregnant woman whose days to give birth have come but doesn't have the strength to do so, the channel is not favorable for delivery. Then, labor must be induced by forcing the mother and the womb to bring the baby into the world. It's an often painful process.

God has declared many things in favor of his people, and many brothers have dreams and visions. They have prophecies and words from God hanging over their lives, but they aren't doing what they should. They sleep and think that everything will happen without their cooperation in applying spiritual principles. That's not how it works in a spiritual battle: we are at war against the forces of darkness. Victory is certain and is ours, but we have to force it by prayer and, if possible, with fasting. This was the approach Daniel took, and he wanted to see the freedom and independence of his people.

The Holy Bible says that while he was praying, on the twenty- first day, the angel came, "Suddenly, a hand touched me, which made me tremble on my knees and on the palms of my hands. And he said to me, "O Daniel, man greatly beloved, understand the words that I speak to you, and stand upright, for I have now been sent to you." While he was speaking this word to me, I stood trembling. Then he said to me, "Do not fear, Daniel, for from the first day that you set your heart to understand and to humble yourself before your God, your words were heard; and I have come because of your word" (Daniel 10:10-12 NKJV).

Daniel fasted for twenty-one days, and the angel couldn't reach Daniel until the twenty-first day. And he told him that the twenty days he fasted weren't necessary because he was sent from the first day Daniel set out to pray.

Now, why didn't this angel make it on the first day? What was in his way that barred those twenty days, too many? What happened? In verse 13, the angel clarifies, "But the prince of the kingdom of Persia withstood me twenty-one days; and behold, Michael, one of the chief princes, came to help me, for I had been left alone there with the kings of Persia."

This is an angel of God saying that he had been barred from bringing an answer to Daniel for twenty-one days. Do you see how these princes of darkness and their powers operate in the heavenly places? Even to the point of blocking (barring) an angel of God! This fact shows how great of an influence they have in the spirit world over events on earth. And this is not a human being speaking; this is an angel narrating his missionary journey to God.

Note that at that time, in the Old Testament, most people had no clear revelation of who Satan was. And because of this lack of clear revelation, God wanted to show them the character and alterations of the devil through certain people who characterized him and over whom was the devil's influence.

The ancient Pharaoh of Egypt, for instance, was a representative and symbolic figure of the devil. What does the devil look like? He is stubborn; when he leaves someone, he wants to come back again. The same happened with Pharaoh: he let the people of Israel out of Egypt but then went after them with chariots and war horses to make them return to slavery and kill some. This attitude reveals the devil's character and his *modus operandi*.

God used repressive regimes to show that behind them is the devil, ruling through them. Regimes where there is no freedom, peace, rights, or privacy for people. Regimes of terror, fear, oppression, where there is no love for human life. Anti-Christian regimes. History has such records in its annals. You must be intelligent enough to observe, study and discern when these kinds of operations occur: you will know when the devil is behind it.

In Daniel's case, God used the prince of the kingdom of Persia. Notice that the Holy Bible doesn't speak of a soldier of Persia, but of the "prince of Persia," and this was a ruler - an emperor, but behind him was a prince of darkness, power and these here are spiritual rulers in the heavenly places, who control physical territories on earth. Now, who came to the aid of the angel who the prince of Persia stopped? Michael - the archangel who fights on behalf of God's people, so the angel's words attest, "But I will tell you what is noted in the Scripture of Truth. (No one upholds me against these, except Michael your prince" (Daniel 10:21 NKJV). If Michael is our prince who, from God, fights on behalf of God's people fighting their spiritual battles, the prince of darkness also has his human representatives who impose their wills on other people. Therefore, as a Church, we have no choice but to pray. We empower our prince and weaken the spiritual prince of darkness and his influence over his human agents by praying.

The angel said to Daniel, "Do you know why I have come to you? And now I must return to fight with the prince of Persia; and when I have gone forth, indeed the prince of Greece will come" (Daniel 10:20 NKJV).

A series of five governmental representatives would have to come into the world before Jesus came here to earth, from the Babylonian empire, the Medes, Persia, Greece, and Rome. When these princes of darkness operate at their peak, they can even move and dictate the direction the whole world must go, in a kind of one world order.

There will be such a thing on earth called the "New World Order," and there will be a single currency of international transactions outside of the current one in place. There will be new forms of commercial transactions that will try to suspend physical money in favor of digital money. The world will see unprecedented things in these last days: there will be so much tribulation, but the church will have already been raptured by Jesus, allowing the devil to place the beast's mark on human beings. The church is the one who prevents the antichrist now because of her continuous prayers and because we are carriers of the Holy Spirit. The church's presence on earth preserves humanity because we are the salt of the earth and the light of the world. There will come a time when money will no longer be used as we see it today; people will be put a mark of the beast on their foreheads and hands so that they can eventually buy and sell.

Many Christians think that the beast's mark is 666, but it won't be like that: it will be scientific and more technological than many imagine. The Antichrist will be a political-religious ruler who will unite the whole world in a New World Order. And anyone who doesn't have this mark will not be able to buy or sell in the marketplace; he will be killed. At that time, the Church will have been raptured to be with the Lord in the air at the imminent coming of the Lord Jesus Christ. Behold, He is coming with the clouds: believe it; the Lord is coming again.

The Antichrist will offer a temporary peace to Israel, and that war in Palestine will stop for some time, at which point he will help Israel build the third temple. He will then allow Israel to return to offering the same sacrifices they offered in the Old Testament. But he will then desecrate the temple and portray himself as Christ seeking worship, and when the Jews discover this, he will want to annihilate Israel in the war of Armageddon. Still, Christ will come to the rescue of Jacob's sons and, with the breath of his mouth, will annihilate the antichrist and the false prophet after the war of Gog and Magog. They will unite against the Lord, but they will be completely defeated.

The antichrist we hear about in the Bible will not be merely a religious figure. Instead, it will be a political figure who will seek to command and dominate the entire world in a New World Order, in a kind of global government - unifying all countries of the world under his political-economic-religious aegis.

Today, in Israel, Jews are preparing to restart temple activities in the Mosaic fashion, with robes as Moses's time. This clerical class is trained to offer sacrifices as they did in the Old Testament, in the temple.

Now, the Antichrist will rule the world in the absence of the Church for seven years. He will have three and a half years of false peace, but the last three years will be severe, and there will be such wickedness and suffering on earth as has not been seen since the earth was created. Daniel was shown this in the seventy-two weeks prophesied by him.

As I mentioned in the previous lines, the antichrist will come in and desecrate the temple and will want to be worshiped as God. In this, the Jews will rebel against him and call him the antichrist. He will want to force them to have the beast's mark.

You know where I stop and wonder? When we speak of the beast, many brothers think of a literal, merely physical animal. "Beast" in the apocalyptic context is not an animal; the name "beast" represents the characteristics of an animal, but it's not the beast itself that is spoken of, although it behaves that way.

CHAPTER XXIII

The danger of making pacts with the devil

I have long taught that the Holy Bible is not a religious book, that the devil is not a religious entity, and that God is not religious. It's about kingdoms, kings, princes, dominions, governments, powers. What makes religion a part of the devil's rituals: killing goats, sheep, and many other things.

For example, although Jesus defeated Satan on the cross, he still boasts and exercises power over many people, including believers who permit him. How? By killing animals and offering their blood in sacrifice, thinking that they are offering masses to their grandfathers and ancestors. This blood is drunk by demons, for they like to drink blood. When masses offer the blood of either animals or birds, this act in itself seals a covenant, that is, an alliance with Satan. From this moment and act, generational ties are established between Satan and this family, and consequently, people begin to suffer, have their lives hindered, and early deaths occur without explanation. Why? Because the devil comes to demand blood. He may even offer a false and temporary illusion (image) of power, fame, and prosperity in business. He may also work with huge material goods in exchange for the suffering of family members: some become barren, others mad, some homeless, and others wandering through life with no direction.

There is always a high price to pay when dealing with the devil. He is not a friend but rather a tenacious enemy of human beings. If you offer him bird and animal blood on one occasion, he will come back demanding human blood, and annual or seasonal deaths will happen in that family. This is why you see people in the newspaper headlines who are happy and prosperous in covetable positions and social status. Still, deep in their hearts, with the lights out and alone, they are suffering or dreaming. They are constantly afflicted and tormented by the demons resulting from the pacts. Some even think of committing suicide, and others, when they smell death, hand over other family members to succumb in their place. Usually, the people handed over are treated as special, and they don't know that they are sheep for the slaughter. No one has ever told these people that the devil doesn't let anything go cheap: everything he gives with one hand, he then comes and takes away with the other, leaving the person destroyed and broke. The devil doesn't let people enjoy what they give. People's ambition and greed mixed with lack of love lead them to adrift in the pacts they make with Satan.

Some even offer their own blood on the devil's altar. Blood gives legality to the devil because it represents life, the life of the people who must die for him to be allowed to operate in favor of those who invite him. The higher the degree or position to be desired, the greater the sacrifice and its consequences. Some are even forced to be licked by snakes and present themselves naked on graves and in cemeteries or huts or in the sea, where the rituals are performed. For fame, ambition and power, people will submit themselves to anything, in the view that it doesn't matter the means to achieve the ends. They become insensitive to the suffering of others, without pity or compassion. They can use any place for this purpose.

It's dangerous to trade or befriend Satan. The apostle Peter described it this way, "Be sober, be vigilant; because your adversary the devil walks about like a roaring lion, seeking whom he may devour. Resist him, steadfast in the faith, knowing that the same sufferings are experienced by your brotherhood in the world" (1 Peter 5:8-9 NKJV).

Notice this verse, "But I will tell you what is noted in the Scripture of Truth. (No one upholds me against these, except Michael your prince" (Daniel 10:21 NKJV).

There are seven angels in Heaven; each of these angels commands a legion of God's angels. God never has and will never fight with the devil. Whenever there is a battle, it's not God; it's his angels because the devil has no power to stand against God.

CHAPTER XXIV

Princes of the Kingdom of Light versus princes of the Kingdom of Darkness

So, seven angels in heaven command other angels; these are heavenly departments that work for God here on earth. These are princes of light who work on behalf of God's good interests on earth. They work on behalf of God's people.

For example, you may have heard of the Archangel Gabriel. This is the Archangel of Heaven or messenger of good news. That means that every time he appears here on earth or one of the angels he commands comes to earth, they only come to bring good news. So, for example, he is the one who appeared to Mary telling her about the birth of Jesus.

Then there is Archangel Michael. This is the commander of the army of God's angels, and every time he appears on earth, it's often to wage war against the hosts of evil. Why did the angel who appeared to Daniel ask Archangel Michael for military support? Because he wasn't a war angel, although he could fight as well. Military-spiritual discipline and the alignment of his status are done with extreme observance.

CHAPTER XXV

Angelic hierarchy

Now, you must understand that among the angels, there are also hierarchies and working codes. For example, before Christ died on the cross, even the Archangel Michael once had a confrontation with the devil disputing about the body of Moses when he died. Yet, the Holy Scripture says, " did not himself dare to condemn him for slander but said, "The Lord rebuke you!" (Jude 1:9 NIV). Why did he proceed in this manner? Because he had no permission, he only had it when Christ died on the cross and dethroned the devil.

"And war broke out in heaven: Michael and his angels fought with the dragon, and the dragon and his angels fought…And they overcame him by the blood of the Lamb and by the word of their testimony, and they did not love their lives to the death" (Revelations 12:7,11 NKJV).

One will wonder how this angel who appeared to Daniel was stopped by the prince of the kingdom of Persia, knowing angels also have power?

Understand that all of God's angels are endowed with superpowers. However, each angel has a mission. In Heaven, things are organized: no angel does another's mission randomly. So, for example, a war angel won't come to give good news in the place of another angel; it's not his job.

So, this particular angel says that he was hindered and couldn't get down, so he had to ask Archangel Michael for backup. Michael doesn't work alone; he also has angels of his order of jurisdiction. He is like an army general who has other officers, sergeants, and soldiers in his sub-units his orders: the Navy command or the Naval Force, the

Infantry fighting on foot, the Air Force, and in some countries, like the States, are creating the Space Force. They are all part of a country's army and have an organized chain of command. Depending on the type of warfare and the strategies to be used in the military counterintelligence in the enemy's camp, the type of force unit to be sent may stand out. God is sapient and omniscient, a strategist extraordinaire, and has his army also highly organized.

The same can happen in the General Police Command, for example. There are cases where the police face a gang of bandits who present themselves with an almost superior apparatus. They, in this case, have to ask the army for help because it's a superior force and prepared for more combative battles.

Even within the police force, some sub-units deal with various issues and problems on behalf of a nation or state. In Mozambique, for example, of the various units that exist there are the Civil Protection Police, Traffic Police, Border Guard Police, and we have the Rapid Reaction Force unit, the R.R.F.

For example: when there is a situation where the R.R.F is deployed to deal with the case, it's expected that there will be smoke there because this force doesn't come with a subpoena or conversation; they come to defuse riots, like riot police.

However, when it's a situation that requires the Civil Protection Police, they are more lenient: they first ask who the defendant is, and have a search and arrest warrant, and take the defendant back to the prison cells, awaiting the legal processes of the Attorney General's Office and the courts. They have to identify themselves with their police card. The R.R.F. doesn't come with a wallet; it comes with a baton and tear gas because it's assumed that there will be resistance.

When Archangel Michael comes, he comes to fight. When he faces battles, you can say, "LORD, send Michael to me..." And when Michael comes, no demon is left standing; they are all knocked down and scattered like the wind scatters chaff.

This angel that we read about in the book of Daniel, where was he stopped? In the highest.

Imagine if someone thought that here, we aren't talking about angels and powers, but about the king or prince of Persia, a human being; how could a human king be able to fly into space and prevent an angel from coming to earth? It's more than clear that this is a spiritually angelic being. It's a reference to one of the princes of darkness, the powers, the devil.

It's common that a person or even the reader of this book has prayed, asking God for a job, marriage, children, among other things, and He sends angels carrying these blessings to you. Then, however, there is a delay because the angels may be fighting for you on the highest.

Dear reader, it's likely that right now, there is a battle going on in the heavenly places on your behalf, in answer to your prayers. You have prayed for your husband or wife, for your children, and right now, battles are going on in the spiritual arena to make what you have asked for happen.

Do you understand now the reason why God requires us to pray? Because if you don't pray, the angels will have no legal right to battle for you, even though you have power. In the spiritual arena, angels don't act like human beings; they don't overstep their action jurisdiction.

This is why we read in the book of Job 2:2 that the devil went up to Heaven, where God is, amid the angels. So why didn't they stop him?

Remember that, in the previous chapters, I mentioned the book of Genesis, chapter six (6), where I told you about the sons of God who married the daughters of men? Now, the expression "sons of God" there doesn't necessarily mean "human beings"; it refers to angels. Angels have also attributed the status of sons of God, but with an angelic body.

Understand that the human being, in the beginning, wasn't a child of God; he was a child of Adam because we came from Adam. We inherited the physical body traits from Adam; what God gave us was the spirit.

Studying the Holy Bible, you won't find the reference of God as being "Father of flesh"; He is called "The Father of spirits," according to Hebrews 12:9. But in the book of Jeremiah 32:27, the Scripture says, " Behold, I am the LORD, the God of all flesh. Is there anything too hard for Me?" Other versions use the term "mankind" in place of the word "flesh." It's very easy to understand this, given Jesus' words in John 4:24, when he said, " God is Spirit, and those who worship Him must worship in spirit and truth." We only became children of God because of Jesus Christ.

The text of John 1:12 confirms this when it says, "But as many as received Him, to them He gave the right to become children of God, to those who believe in His name."

This is why in the Old Testament, no one called God "Father" but used various attributes of Him, most prominently "*Yahweh* or Jehovah, the LORD," among others. To this day, Jews use the expression "*Hashem*" "the name" a lot to avoid pronouncing His name "*Yahweh*" because, according to them, this name is too holy for our impure lips to pronounce it. However, we Christians (by belonging to the New Testament) call him "Father" now because of Jesus Christ. Therefore, the apostle John exclaimed, "See what great love the Father has lavished on us, that we should be called children of God! And that is what we are! The reason the world does not know us is that it did not know him" (1 John 3:1 NIV). This is the experience and privilege of New Testament believers because of the blood of Jesus.

Who were the "children of God" in the old days? They were the angels

Have a look at this Scripture:

"On another day the angels came to present themselves before the Lord, and Satan also came with them to present himself before him. And the Lord said to Satan, "Where have you come from?" Satan answered the Lord, "From roaming throughout the earth, going back and forth on it" (Job 2:1-2 NIV).

We can notice, based on this Scripture, that in Heaven, there is gradation: the angels go there and present themselves and receive missions, then come to earth to execute the divine missions and return to Heaven to present again. This is wonderful! The Kingdom of God is very organized, the spirit world is organized, God is organized, and the devil is also organized. However, the devil likes to disorganize people's lives on earth. But Jesus came to reorganize them for us. So you must develop the spirit of prayer.

When you pray, angels will be sent by God to patrol your yard, your neighborhood, your zone, and won't let demons move freely there. Your house will become an air restriction zone for demons, witches, and wizards.

Chapter XXVI

Victory confessions

Every night before you go to bed, you can pray like this, "Father, I pray tonight that God's angels will patrol my neighborhood, my block and that no demons or wizards will fly over this zone, in the name of Jesus. I declare the backyard of my house and my neighborhood "No fly zone," meaning air restriction zone for all demons and wizards. No demons will fly over it, no powers, no principalities can fly here, in the name of Jesus. My family and I lie down like carefree babies and have good dreams in the name of Jesus. I release the ministry of the angels now on behalf of this place. God's angels are surrounding this house and this neighborhood now. Demonic activities in this area are sealed off, in the name of Jesus." You can extend the prayer to the whole city, province, or state you are in. This is how you neutralize demonic activity in an area: by praying and enacting words of authority in the name of Jesus Christ.

Through prayer, you practically control and protect the whole neighborhood at night until everyone sleeps well in that neighborhood. It's because you are in that neighborhood that everyone sleeps well. In a family home, if there is a mother who prays, the children sleep peacefully, and because there is a father who prays, the family sleeps peacefully, in the name of Jesus.

When the angels of God, in answer to the believer's prayer, patrol the territory or spiritual area in which the children of God are, the wizards are informed that in this country, there is a neighborhood and a block where there is someone who prevents them from flying over it. Oh glory, hallelujah!

At the wizards and witches' meeting, their boss stands up with the agenda for the night, including the map of the territory to be attacked, the number of houses that have to be invaded, and the gallons of human blood to be drunk. And he says, "There is an area in this province, in whose neighborhood and one block are protected by the blood of Jesus; I am telling you demons that when you fly there, please use your spiritual G.P.S. well. Your coordinates must not be missed because if by mistake you fall into that house where those Christians are, you will come back without wings. There is a lot of fire there. They pray a lot." This often happens in the spirit world. That's why you wake up in the morning and hear your neighbor saying that your neck is sore, and another neighbor says that you didn't sleep well because of these kinds of spiritual attacks. But don't worry, your home has been marked and protected by the blood of Jesus.

Know that there are relatives of yours who don't even go to church, but they sleep well because of the prayer you say, and they don't even know it; they think they are smart.

Every day in the spirit world, how many liters of blood are to be drunk on the roads and highways is planned. The demons are distributed in countries, provinces, and zones by the principalities, powers, and princes of darkness and are sent out to work day and night.

However, wherever the children of the Kingdom of God are, they cannot attack, and many people are protected by being on the same bus or plane where a praying Christian is. The believer who prays creates liberated spiritual zones where demonic activities are restricted. This is why a person may not prosper in an area controlled by the princes of darkness and powers but may be able to leave and go and live in another spiritually liberated area, city, province, state, or country. And when you get there, the atmosphere is light, you feel at peace, your potential is unleashed, and your life begins to prosper in every way. You feel as if you have just been released from prison. Yes, sometimes you have to move from one region to another to be successful. Otherwise, you have to be spiritually strong and release the territory.

When evil spirits find this out, they try to intensify their attacks against you. Even you may start to be accused of things you haven't done and have your name smeared, just so you don't get ahead. These spirits can use people and manipulate laws. They can raise up people to persecute you without just cause. Since they are princes of darkness, they usually attack people's minds, blocking them from having significant initiatives or going beyond the general status quo. They often release sorcery and witchcraft, which block a person's potential and can even track them spiritually, diverting the good things that would happen to them. They can use people to hinder the development of a region, attacking those who bring initiatives for progress. Usually, hatred, envy, and sorcery are the order of the day, and many people are initiated into these demonic activities.

But son/daughter of God, don't be afraid, for we have full authority over them by the blood and name of our Lord Jesus Christ. Therefore, the psalmist assured, "You will not fear the terror of night, nor the arrow that flies by day, nor the pestilence that stalks in the darkness, nor the plague that destroys at midday. A thousand may fall at your side, ten thousand at your right hand, but it will not come near you. No harm will overtake you, no disaster will come near your tent" (Psalm 91:5-7,10 NIV). We are protected, glory be to God, for the Lord is our refuge, our fortress, and in him, we trust. I advise you to meditate on the entire chapter of Psalm 91 and personalize the psalmist's words in the first person in prayer.

CHAPTER XXVII

Neutralizing evil operations and stopping the princes of the
darkness in the spiritual arena

❝Then the LORD said to Satan, "Have you considered my servant Job?
There is no one on earth like him; he is blameless and upright, a
man who fears God and shuns evil. And he still maintains his integrity,
though you incited me against him to ruin him without any reason."
"Skin for skin!" Satan replied. "A man will give all he has for his own
life" (Job 2:3-4 NIV).

It's a wonder how the devil managed to deceive the angels. He
came into their midst and walked with them, and they thought he was
one of them.

Here was a conversation taking place in heaven about the life of
a person who was on earth. Job couldn't hear what was being said, but
plans were being made there.

The devil said to God, "But now stretch out your hand and strike
his flesh and bones, and he will surely curse you to your face" (Job 2:5
NIV).

So, Job got sick, and that sickness wasn't natural. Now, imagine
that in Job's day, there were clinics, and he went there and said that he
just had that disease. According to science, the doctors would probably
have given him medication when the actual cause (spiritual) escaped
them since the illness was planned in the spiritual arena.

The devil plans in the spirit and only looks for human means to
execute what he has planned. Hence, when he wants to steal, he uses
someone (a human agent) to accomplish his mission. So likewise, he

uses specific means, either spiritual, material, or even human, when he wants to kill.

It's common for someone to complain of heartache and to die soon. What happened? An arrow was spiritually shot and pierced the heart of the unprotected person. Hence why in spiritual combat, we are encouraged to wear the breastplate of righteousness. Where? On the chest. What for? To protect that area from all attacks or fiery darts of the evil one.

The Scripture urges us to put on the whole spiritual armor: the helmet of salvation to protect the head region, the breastplate of righteousness to protect the chest region, gird the loins with the truth, which is the Word of God to be ready for a battle at any moment, and wear on your feet the gospel of salvation to create progress, and save others. Another part of the most crucial armor involves the shield of faith to quench the fiery darts that the devil may send. "I refuse to get sick, in the name of Jesus. No one will die prematurely in my family this year, in the name of Jesus. I refuse to be poor because the grace of Christ is in me. I refuse to be afraid because greater is the Spirit of God who is in me than the forces of darkness and spiritual hosts of wickedness that operate in the world." Therefore, you must stand firm at all times. The same Scripture also recommends us to use the sword of the Spirit, which is the Word of God. You must study the Word of God, keep it in your heart, and use it as a weapon of war in your mouth. It's like a two-edged sword: it will cut through all evil and destroy the devil's walls, opening paths for you to progress in life. (Read Ephesians 6:12-18; Hebrews 4:12). Find a more detailed exposition in my book, "The Good Fight of Faith: How to Fight and Win: Secrets of constant victories in spiritual battles." It will bless you immensely.

Over the following few chapters, I will give you prayer points and more strategies for stopping and neutralizing the diabolical actions of wickedness by these spiritual beings. However, we need to decode the identity of angels in the Old Testament texts. So, let's look in-depth at the "sons of God" issue in reference to angels and not to human beings. In the Old Testament, human beings were not, roughly speaking, called "sons of God." Why? Because the sphere of human beings' domain was the earth, while these angels had to act in the heavenly places. God gave the earth to man and said, "have dominion over it and subdue it. " (Genesis 1:26-28)

Have a look at these passages again:

"One day the angels came to present themselves before the LORD, and Satan also came with them. The LORD said to Satan, "Where have you come from?" Satan answered the LORD, "From roaming throughout the earth, going back and forth on it." Then the LORD said to Satan, "Have you considered my   servant Job? There is no one on earth like him; he is blameless and upright, a man who fears God and shuns evil." "Does Job fear God for nothing?" Satan replied. "Have you not put a hedge around him and his household and everything he has? You have blessed the work of his hands so that his flocks and herds are spread throughout the land. But now stretch out your hand and strike everything he has, and he will surely curse you to your face" (Job 1:6-11 NIV).

Note that the devil can go from Africa to Europe in less than 1 second, circling the earth. There are no physical boundaries for him and his agents because they are spirits. This conversation was taking place between God and Satan on high, in a sphere called the "spirit world," where man has no access in his physical state, save (except) for his spirit.

Did you know that there are conversations to be had in the spirit right now about you? It's serious! You only see the consequences of things you don't even know where they started.

God told the devil that he could roam the earth, but he had to watch his Servant Job. Job's life attracted God. This is how the Holy Scripture describes him, "...this man was blameless and upright; he feared God and shunned evil" (Job 1:1 NIV).

Beloved brother or sister:

1. **Can God, in Heaven, now brag about you and your life?**

2. **Does He have any positive reports about you?**

3. **What do you think God would be commenting about you now?**

Job had a good report, "a sincere man, and upright, and God-fearing, and turning aside from evil." His character counts a lot, for he has to glorify God.

Now, well, for a long time, Satan had been trying to destroy Job's life, but he couldn't because God had put a fence around him, a wall of protection. Only Job didn't know that he was protected. That is why he was always worried and afraid that something wrong would happen to him and/or his children. And it was this constant worry and permanent fear that broke through the wall of protection that God had placed for him so that the devil wouldn't bite him. Note Job's words, " What I feared has come upon me; what I dreaded has happened to me. I have no peace, no quietness; I have no rest, but only turmoil" (Job 3:25-26 NIV). Find the detailed explanation on this subject in my book "Do Not Break the Wall" You will live free from fear and be aware of the divine protection over you.

When you always live worried and afraid, what you fear is what will happen to you. Fear is a negative force that attracts negative things. Faith is a positive force that attracts positive energies. Faith comes by hearing the Word of God, and fear comes by hearing the words of this world fabricated by the devil. Don't be afraid.

Fear is one of the devil's greatest weapons. When you are afraid of something, there is a high probability of it happening. That is why God repeats, "Fear not" (Isaiah 41:10).

Even when things seem contrary, don't be afraid. Keep trusting God. SAY: I refuse to be afraid, in the name of Jesus.

God only took away the fence that was over Job when he opened the doors to the devil. The Scripture warns, "Whoever digs a pit may fall into it; whoever breaks through a wall may be bitten by a snake" (Ecclesiastes 10:8 NIV).

In one day, look at what happened to Job when he lost his wall of protection. "One day, when Job's sons and daughters were feasting and drinking wine at the oldest brother's house, a messenger came to Job and said, "The oxen were plowing, and the donkeys were grazing nearby, and the Sabeans attacked and made off with them. They put the servants to the sword, and I am the only one who has escaped to tell you" (Job 1:13-15 NIV).

CHAPTER XXVIII

Gradation of the diabolic attacks and Job's suffering

First: Job lost his livestock, his farm, his business: his animals died, and ninety-nine percent (99%) of his shepherds died

Second: their ten children will die: three boys and seven girls

Third: your skin has been attacked by a scab

In light of the above, we can categorize the devil's attacks on Job's life into three areas, namely:

Business/ professional destruction (enterprises): Job's company was destroyed.

We note this from the report of the loss of his farm and livestock. At the time, the economy was more farming and accumulation of gold and silver. All of this was affected in one day.

Labor Destruction: death of your workers (employees): Job's workers were killed, except for the one who came to give him the news.

Family destruction: His children died in a windstorm that brought down the event hall where they were staying, and his marriage was also negatively affected, given the woman's frailty in dealing with difficult moments in life: living without employees, without benefits, and without the company of her children, aggravated by her husband's sickly medical condition, due to which both couldn't touch each other or relate intimately as husband and wife. As if this were not enough, his relationship with his friends takes a new turn: separation and dissension in belief.

Spiritual analysis

Dear reader, I'm showing you the consequences of diabolical plans against men. I'm showing you that we, here on earth, only see things happening without knowing the cause.

Looking at all this misery that happened to Job, what does it symbolize or represent? Economic and financial crisis. This is because, having that livestock and farm, he could sell it for gold and silver. Therefore, the Holy Bible says that Job was wealthy. At that time, wealth was configured in three categories: wealth in cattle, in gold and silver, or wealth in agricultural terms, as I explained earlier.

However, here, Job's economy and his workers were severely affected by a decision made in the spirit. Do you see the gravity of these things?

CHAPTER XXIX

Associated causes

Natural and human agencies instrumentalized by the devil for evil

Verse 16 says, "While he was still speaking, another messenger came and said, "The fire of God fell from the heavens and burned up the sheep and the servants, and I am the only one who has escaped to tell you."

What do we see here? Fire, natural calamities.

If fire came, or there was a fire now, and it burned the houses in your neighborhood, in a phenomenological study, what would you describe this phenomenon as? Natural calamity, forest fire.

To say that even what are commonly called natural calamities, such as tsunamis, earthquakes, cyclones, torrential rain, hurricane, windstorms, etc., many of these things are caused by demons. But people say it's something natural. It's not always natural. There are spiritual forces of evil behind it.

Hence why you can live in a country, or a city, where they say there will be a hurricane next week, and you can pray and cancel the hurricane, and nothing happens.

Dear reader, I'm showing you that certain things that happen in our daily lives are not normal. The bulk of them is spiritually planned. If you can control them from the spiritual world, you will prevent them from affecting you negatively in the physical world.

If you were Job, and you saw your livestock dying in a single day, what assessment would you make? What would you say? He would probably say that he is unlucky or that the animals were affected by the flu.

Even certain outbreaks of disease and epidemics have resulted from the actions of demons and the devil's fallen, angels. For this reason, as a son or daughter of God, you need to be in constant prayer and make prophetic decrees in the spiritual arena, "I live in this neighborhood and command it by the Word of God and prayer. I'm in charge, reigning with Christ, and no force of darkness will prevail in this place. I neutralize every arrow launched against my family and this neighborhood, in the name of Jesus." Thus, you can force spatial spiritual order and tranquility by prayer and prophetic decrees.

Verse seventeen (17) of the book of Job, chapter 1, says, "While he was still speaking, another messenger came and said, "The Chaldeans formed three raiding parties and swept down on your camels and made off with them. They put the servants to the sword, and I am the only one who has escaped to tell you."

Each of the surviving servants of Job's servants was narrating his painful experience, and still speaking, came another with his ordeal. Each one of Job's possessions, his farm, and livestock were dying and were being taken away by diabolical action.

All this was happening in the blink of an eye, on the same day, at the same hour. Each of his servants was coming with bad news, some more serious than the others.

That's where the first TV news started. When you watch TV news for thirty minutes, analyze it well, and you will realize that ninety percent of the information is negative in many cases. While they should be announcing good things, because there are many good things that governments or good citizens are doing, but it never appears. Instead of informing, always considering both sides of the coin: the occurrence of good things and the unpleasant ones, the focus, consciously or unconsciously of the newsrooms, has been to increase fear and cause panic in people's hearts. Bias also counts in these processes, and that is why if you don't study the Word of God, you can live with your heart in your hands: always apprehensive and afraid. Instead of being an informed citizen, you become uninformed and misguided, unable to discern and distinguish truth from lies. As if he were an acephalous consumer. The devil likes this because he operates by fear and deception. He is the father of lies. Therefore, it's necessary to read the letters of the words and the informational trends.

For example, news about Africa is usually portrayed with images of wars, famines, diseases, misery, and crime, as if they were primitive sub-humans.

When one is in Europe and sees news about Africa, it's common to see only those suburbs, where people don't even have clothes, and say that this is Africa. You should also take pictures of the cities, the well-dressed people, the beaches, and tourist places, and portray the beauty of humanity and nature that this continent has. Because otherwise, given the emphasis on the unworthy aspects of a human being, some people might even be afraid to travel or visit these 54 countries. This is why many people think that in Africa, there are only miserable and unclothed people living in the bush with or like animals, eating giraffe meat and being devoured by lions. Even children who don't eat become newspaper headlines.

However, there are many well-nourished children too, and this is not just the fault of those externally making the news either; some places present this image to attract support and donations. There is a need for a change in approach and mindset for the good of all humanity.

On the day of Job's trial, Satan was controlling the media and information Jesus said, "The poor you will always have with you, but you will not always have me" (Matthew 26:11 NIV). The poor are the sea where the rich swim.

For many, just by seeing a group of poor people, they do a social project, when in fact, they don't want to help. They just want the money for their pockets. Then they use that same money to make mansions and buy luxury cars. This isn't bad, as long as it's not the fruit of the exploitation of the poor but of the dignified work of each one. As the Scripture says, "The worker deserves his wages" (1 Timothy 5:18b NIV).

Bad news flooded Job's day, for whom in the previous day, everything seemed peaceful until he broke through the wall that protected him and let himself be bitten by the serpent.

The narrative continues in verses 18-19, "While he was still speaking, yet another messenger came and said, "Your sons and daughters were feasting and drinking wine at the oldest brother's house when suddenly a mighty wind swept in from the desert and struck the four corners of the house. It collapsed on them, and they are dead, and I am the only one who has escaped to tell you."

Sudden Deaths in the Family

When the devil found his free run, he began to attack Job's life, peeling him off on all sides. Suddenly, many people begin to die in one day.

Now, note that this diversity of crises in Job's life: economic-financial crisis, work crisis, and immediate death of members of his family and his workers, were not the result of merely natural acts; they were planned in the spiritual world and executed in the physical.

Who planned the death of Job's children and his collaborators? Satan. Was it Satan who executed them? No.

This man's report says that a wind came and hit the house where they were, the house fell down and they died. Notice that he is blaming the wind- the windstorm -because that is what he can naturally observe.

Job's animals, that is, his livestock? One part died, and the Chaldeans stole another part. They blamed the Chaldeans. If Job had to go to physical war, who would he be fighting with? Those men (the Chaldeans) weren't the primary cause of all this misfortune. "But as an apostle?" - you may wonder. Well, God's Word explains, "For our struggle is not against flesh and blood, but against the rulers, against the authorities, against the powers of this dark world and against the spiritual forces of evil in the heavenly realms" (Ephesians 6:12 NIV).

Now, do you understand why the war is not physical, even though whoever executes the diabolical plan may be a physical agent? Who sold Jesus Christ? Judas. What does the Bible say about Judas? "Then Satan entered Judas" (Luke 22:3 NIV).

Who had Christ handed over to be crucified? The Jews - the then clerical class jealous of his ministry. But Jesus said to them, "You belong to your father, the devil, and you want to carry out your father's desires. He was a murderer from the beginning, not holding to the truth, for there is no truth in him. When he lies, he speaks his native language, for he is a liar and the father of lies" (John 8:44 NIV).

Understand that behind every negative action of men are demons - spiritual forces of evil; and behind every good action of men are God's messenger angels and the Holy Spirit.

The activities that take place on earth today, whether good or bad, are influenced by the spirit world.

Prayer, faith, and the Word of God are the shields we have to use.

Chapter XXX

Faith is a protection shield

By faith, you can say, "In the name of Jesus, the greatest is in me, I refuse to be sick, my body is a temple of the Holy Spirit; no one will die in my family this year. I declare protection over my home, co-workers, workers, or my employers and their families. Satan is defeated; he has no power over me; every tool forged against me will not prosper in the name of Jesus. I refuse to succumb to his clutches. I break them now. Fear has no place in me. One must behave manfully, like a good soldier of Christ – always ready to fight spiritually. As God told Joshua, "No one will be able to stand against you all the days of your life. As I was with Moses, I will be with you; I will never leave you or forsake you. Be strong and courageous, because you will lead these people to inherit the land I swore to their ancestors to give them" (Joshua 1:5-6 NIV). Strengthen yourself in the Lord and in the power of his might. He is with you every day.

Here's my question to you: If plans were being made now, in the spirit, and in the camp of the enemy against you, would you know it? Probably not, because they are happening in the spiritual arena.

Based on what I have taught you about Job, can you understand the correlation between diabolical plans and human activity here on earth?

Ask yourself: Where am I, spiritually?

You must understand that in Christ, we are not victims, but champions, because the devil, although organized and administratively structured, is an eternally defeated enemy.

Repeat these words, "The devil is an eternally defeated enemy. He and his demons are defeated, defeated. Satan is defeated. Jesus has won, and the devil has been defeated and disarmed. He has nothing on me."

With all that I have taught you here, I have explained how the devil operates together with his powers. Keep in mind that, although he is evil, he has been defeated. The devil has been hobbled in his legs and hands; the blood of Jesus has paralyzed him over those who are saved - those who are in Christ. He has no power over you, but he has it over those who are disconnected from Jesus Christ.

The apostle vindicated this reality when he said, "We know that we are children of God and that the whole world is under the control of the evil one" (1 John 5:19 NIV).

When you are on a bus that is about to crash, start praying like this, "Father, in the name of Jesus, I cancel the devil's evil plan and declare, by the authority of Jesus Christ, that no one will die in this car."

If you are on a plane that is about to crash, and they say the pilot has lost the coordinates, say, "Father, in the name of Jesus, I declare that no one will die on this plane, and break the influence of the devil and his spiritual hosts of wickedness on this aircraft. So release the ministry of the angels." And continue saying, "Satan, get your hands off this aircraft and get away from the psychic state of the pilots, in the name of Jesus."

Do you remember that the apostle Paul was on an utterly wrecked ship on the high seas before reaching an island called Malta when he was shipwrecked? (Read the book of Acts, chapter 28). Each passenger and crew could only save themselves by clinging to one of the wrecks of the ship to reach the shore of the island, where they found dry land.

Now, here is the apostle Paul (a spiritual man) taken prisoner, put with other prisoners on a ship bound for Rome. The ship had the sailor, and the centurion of the guard, who placed the prisoners who were being tied to it, to be tried and imprisoned in Rome. Paul was one of them, albeit innocently.

Paul said to the captain, "Men, I can see that our voyage is going to be disastrous and bring great loss to ship and cargo, and to our own lives also" (Acts 27:10 NIV).

Being a professional sailor, the captain (of the ship) could analyze with his compass the behavior of the sea. Still, Paul could see the diabolical plan about the ship, its crew, and passengers in the spirit.

They wouldn't listen to the voice of God and left. When they reached the high seas, a strong windstorm attacked the ship so that, humanly speaking, there was no way for them to escape. For days, they saw neither the sun nor the stars; they were in the dark.

When the ship was coming apart, the commander in charge of the prisoners wanted to kill them all, but Paul, boldly and trusting in his God, said to them, "But now I urge you to keep up your courage because not one of you will be lost; only the ship will be destroyed. Last night an angel of the God to whom I belong and whom I serve stood beside me and said, 'Do not be afraid, Paul. You must stand trial before Caesar; and God has graciously given you the lives of all who sail with you" (Acts 27:22-24 NIV).

Notice this:

Physically, Paul was in the centurion's hands, but spiritually, the centurion and the men on the ship, from the crew to the passengers, were all in Paul's hands. He was a commander of spiritual territories.

Can you see the difference between the planes here?

On the physical-human plane, Paul was in the centurion's hands, but on the spiritual plane, the commander in charge of the prisoners and the men who were on the ship, to live and find their families again, including the captain of the ship, were all in Paul's hands.

The one who saved them all from dying in the shipwreck was the angel of God. So there was an angelic activity: the angel of God preserved their lives so that they wouldn't die because Paul was there and prayed for them.

You can also intercede for your family and be blessed, protected, preserved, delivered, saved, and prospered because of your prayer.

If some demon appears in a witch and says he's going to kill everyone, in reaction, you say, "No, because I'm here; I cancel death, I neutralize the spirit of death, and no one will die here, in the name of Jesus." So start praying, that prayer that comes out of the heart, mixed with faith.

Seeing your family stagnating sentimentally, you can turn the situation around. With faith and prayer, open your mouth and say, "It's been a long time since anyone has been married in this family. There will be marriages in this family this year. In the name of Jesus, I declare it now." You continue, "It's long past time that no one has their plot of land, their plot of land, and their own house in this family. It's long past time that no one has children, that no one works; I cancel this, in the name of Jesus."

Schedule prayer and fasting, and start fighting in the spirit on behalf of your family. Do like Daniel, who prayed in fasting until the prince of Persia relented. Pray until the powers and hosts of darkness give way and withdraw from your family completely. Pray until the cords that bound your family to these evil spirits are cut. Pray until your home and family are inhospitable places for the devil and his agents. Pray in the name of Jesus. Sow what you want to happen in your family. Pluck out with words what the devil has planted. You have spiritual authority in Christ, and the devil knows it. It's time to use it in faith now. God's Word already predicts the reaction of the devil and his agents: to flee. That is why it encourages, "Therefore submit to God. Resist the devil, and he will flee from you" (James 4:7 NKJV).

You are the light of your family, more than that, you are the light of the world in darkness and the salt of the earth. Make your light shine now, and give your life, your family, state, and nation some flavor as the salt of the earth. The heavens, the angels, and Jesus are on your side. The angels have already been sent to your rescue. So don't let your guard down. Fight the good fight of faith. Make progress in the spirit. I see the power of God being activated in you now. The Holy Spirit is operating in your life, giving you the word and the will to pray. You are being equipped now. No spirit of darkness will prevail against you. You are in the forefront, in charge, using the Word of God, which is the sword of the Spirit, and you are cutting away all evil before you.

Wake up, take control, and stop crying. Confront your fears and chase away all the ghosts of the past. It's time to reign with Christ and put the devil to flight. All the suffering you've had so far is enough.

Now, reverse things in the spirit. Destroy the devil at the wheel who was miserably commanding your family's destinies. It's time to be in green pastures and be led meekly to still waters. It's time to have your soul cooled with peace and quiet. It's time to get the joy back in that face and the smile back in that mouth. It's your jubilee, freedom from bondage, and from the prison of covenants with demons and curses. It's time to preach the Gospel with boldness, signs, and wonders. It's time to conquer spiritual territories and save lives from the clutches and diabolical agenda in the spirit and the physical. It's time to build up the Church of Christ on earth and rescue lost souls. It's time to heal the soul's wounds and start life anew, with good cheer and a good mood. It's time to have your whole family worship the Lord. It's time for restoration and restitution of all that the devil has stolen from you. It's time to raid the demonic banks and warehouses and get back all the goods he has stolen from you since the time of your great-great-great-great- grandfathers. A deliverer has been born into the family: a David, an Esther; a Gideon and a Deborah: that person is you. You cannot fail now. You cannot let yourself be distracted now. This is the time; this is the hour: it's time to shine and glorify the God who created the heavens and the earth. It's time to say, "Your kingdom come. Your will be done here on earth as it is in heaven."

Equipped with the revelations you have received in this book and energized by the Holy Spirit, you can say, "My grandmother died without getting married, my mother also died without getting married, it won't be that way with me. So, Satan, you have to let go of me now, by the blood of Jesus and fire of the Word."

If this is your case, you can also neutralize the spirits of early death in your family: "In this year alone, many have died. My cousins have died, my uncle died, my grandmother died, and now my brother is sick! No, no! Brother, you are not going to die. I cancel this death, let's pray, in the name of Jesus." Pray for your family, "My good one, you will live in the name of Jesus. Satan will not take your soul, no. I will break his influence over you and neutralize every means he tries to use.

None of his tools will prosper. Receive life now in your spirit, your soul, and your body, in the name of Jesus."

Prayerfully continue, "Father, I stand between heaven and earth and declare that my family is set free, blessed and saved, in the name of the Lord Jesus."

Call your sister and tell her, "My dear sister, this year we are each going up the aisle in marriage. Things have changed now, in the spirit." Tell your brother, "Brother; this company is not going to close or go bankrupt. On the contrary, I will get down on my knees, and the company will rise in the name of Jesus. Many companies have gone bankrupt because of the crisis the world is experiencing, but not yours, not ours. Strategies are given to us now, by the Spirit of God for subsequent phases."

Dear reader, you have to take this seriously. These are not fairy tales. I, too, have had to put the devil to flight from my family in the past. There was a time in my family when no one married; even my parents were not officially married. So, armed with these truths that I have revealed to you here, I said, "By the power and grace of God, I'm going to change this." What happened? My older sister got officially married. I got married, my parents got married, my siblings got married, and now everyone has a wedding ring on their ring fingers. Not only them but also part of the extended family. Why?

Because there was a man in the family who said to the devil, "Enough. Go away."

Know that you cannot sleep or nap in the spirit; that is, you must not be distracted or lost. You must not waver. Your enemy, the devil, doesn't play around; he "prowls around like a roaring lion, looking for someone to devour" (1 Peter 5:8 NIV). He isn't looking for you to play video games. He does dirty business but serious business. However, I declare that you and your family are protected.

CONCLUSION

Our place of glory, authority, and power

So far, we have studied the spirit world, its agents, its operations, and how it influences life on earth. We have seen that we have God's angels in the spiritual arena, who represent the forces of good. These have been fighting on behalf of humanity, usually in answer to the prayers of the saints on earth. They also have their hierarchy, their functions, and missions. Furthermore, we have studied God's Word from the Old Testament to the New Testament and have seen that in the spiritual arena, there are also fallen angels of the devil and demons in the heavenly places. They represent the evil forces that negatively dictate the lives of men here on earth. They use a human agency and physical phenomena to perpetrate evil and inflict suffering upon humans. They hate human beings and yearn for their destruction. Although they have an organized structure and function in a hierarchy with a single command board, directed by Satan, they have no power over the believer because they have been defeated and stripped by the Lord Jesus. The Scripture vindicates this by saying that Christ has stripped the principalities and powers. He exposed them publicly and triumphed over them on the cross (Colossians 2:15). Furthermore, Scripture assures us that it's Christ who leads us in triumph every day and causes the aroma of His knowledge to waft through us (2 Corinthians 2:14).

We defined the spirit world by presenting its various synonyms, "spiritual arena, or heavenly places," and said that they are spheres of spiritual activities. God's angels may carry out these activities to further their plans and purposes on behalf of humanity. But they are also fertile spheres for the planning, strategies, and attacks of the forces of darkness. It's against these forces that we wage spiritual combat, hence why the believer must know that we are at war—a war between good and evil, light and darkness.

Despite all this, there is nothing to fear because Jesus has given us the authority. And coincidentally, we too, by virtue of our salvation and unity with Christ, are in the heavenly places, in a position above that of the forces of darkness. Therefore, the layer in which we operate, live, walk, and do things is also spiritual and far superior to that of the devil and his agents.

It's about this position of authority and advantage that I want to talk about in this chapter and leave some food for thought so that, as a child of God, you know who you are, what you have, and where you are in Christ. Then, you can secure and protect your earthly assets and your life from this spiritual and sublime position. It's also from there that you will successfully fight and achieve glorious successes over the devil and every kind of evil. Moreover, from here, you can, with a simple word of faith, create what you want to happen in your life or destroy the works of the devil.

Let us look at this Scripture:

"Do not cease to give thanks for you, making mention of you in my prayers: that the God of our Lord Jesus Christ, the Father of glory, may give to you the spirit of wisdom and revelation in the knowledge of Him, the eyes of your understanding being enlightened; that you may know what is the hope of His calling, what are the riches of the glory of His inheritance in the saints, and what is the exceeding greatness of His power toward us who believe, according to the working of His mighty power which He worked in Christ when He raised Him from the dead and seated Him at His right hand in the heavenly places, far above all principality and power and might and dominion, and every name that is named, not only in this age but also in that which is to come. And He put all things under His feet and gave Him to be head over all things to the church, which is His body, the fullness of Him who fills all in all" (Ephesians 1:16-23 NIV).

In this context, Paul prayed for the brothers of the Church of Ephesus that they would have the spirit of wisdom and revelation. The word "Revelation" comes from the Greek *apokalupsis* and has the sense of taking away the veil and removing the scales to see. It means "to discover" and refers to the state of understanding. This prayer extends to us also, Christians of the 21st century.

Repeat these words out loud, "There is an exceedingly great power of God over me. The power that protects me and covers me is super-excellent. There is a power that protects me. God's power is over me every day. Against this power that protects and guards me, there is no devil; there is no power that can prevail. Jesus Christ is above every power, principality, and demon. And Jesus Christ is my Lord."

Understand that the power in reference in this context, God had never used it before. He began to use it (for the first) time when He raised Christ from the dead. It's called "resurrection power." Of course, in the Old Testament, the dead were raised by God's power in the ministries of Elijah, Elisha, and the prophets. But this macro atomic dimension of power had never been used before. So, those who were resurrected later died, either by age or other circumstances. This power produces eternal life, a life that prevails over all that is corruptible and perishable. This is the power that principalities and powers have not been able to stop or hinder. Jesus went to hell and came out alive; no demon could stop him.

Our privileged place in Christ

Can Jesus be bewitched? No. Can these powers tame him? Also, no. Because He is above them all, and God has subjected all things to His feet.

Are the legs connected to the head or not? They are because Jesus Christ is the head, and we are the body. Where are the demons now, since they cannot be under a head that has no body? Under the feet, whose body is connected to the head.

Therefore, all these princes of darkness, powers, principalities, and spiritual hosts of wickedness in the heavenly places, including the demons, no matter what their hierarchy, function, or type of operations they carry out, are under our feet.

Say with me, "Satan and his demons are under my feet as long as I remain in Christ. Hallelujah!"

Jesus Christ is seated in the heavenly places at the right hand of the Majesty, above all power, every name, all demons, and every name that can be named.

Is He bewitchable? No! Imagine that someone doesn't like Him and wants to curse Him. Can that person go to the wizards or witches and make a potion from harming Him? Absolutely not. Not at all, because Christ is above all powers and entourage.

Now, we will read the text of the Ephesians 2:4-6 (NIV), "But because of his great love for us, God, who is rich in mercy, made us alive with Christ even when we were dead in transgressions — it is by grace you have been saved. And God raised us up with Christ and seated us with him in the heavenly realms in Christ Jesus."

Reread verse six (6), but take out "us" and put in "me." As you reread it, you will be left, "And God raised me up with Christ and seated me with him in the heavenly realms in Christ Jesus."

Questions of spiritual deepening

Keep in mind the form used in the sentence we just read, answer the following questions.

2. Whom did Jesus resurrect? Answer: Me.

1. Where am I now? Answer: I am seated in the heavenly places, in Christ Jesus.

This is a spiritual communication: He says that although your physical body is where you are now, you are spiritually in dominion. Spiritually, you are seated in Christ, in the heavenly places above this hierarchical structure of the kingdom of darkness.

3. So, if there is a set of diabolical plans against you, where are those plans being made? Answer: in heavenly places.

4. And what was the definition we gave of these places? Answer: we said it was a sphere of spiritual activities.

5. And who plans the demonic activities? Answer: it's the devil and his executioners.

6. And you are above or below them? Answer: above them.

Now, imagine that they plan something against you; can they hit you? Answer: no. Because for them to get you here on earth, they will have to have dominion over you in the spirit. But if you have dominion over them in the spirit, they will have no way to get you on earth.

Do you understand the revelation now? Our escape doesn't begin on earth but in heaven and the heavenly places. When they plan evil against us, we first escape in the spirit. And when we escape in the spirit, we automatically disappear from their spiritual map. Consequently, when they come in the physical realm looking for us, they no longer get us. Glory be to God through Jesus Christ! This is why I always say, "Jesus Christ is the same yesterday and today and forever" (Hebrews 13:8).

I would like you to understand this. For that reason, reread verse six (6) as if you were talking to your family. That is, see yourself and your nuclear and/or extended family members included in this place and say, "And raised us up together with him, and made us sit in heavenly places in Christ Jesus."

Repeat with me out loud, "I'm alive and sitting in the heavenly places, in Christ Jesus. There is no bewitching me, no catching me, not today or ever. I'm not even standing; I'm relaxed, seated in Christ."

Now, imagine that someone wants to bewitch you; where do you think they will catch (find) you? Nowhere.

If someone says that there is a wizard who wants to kill you or harm you, say, "Go tell the wizard that I sit above him; he has no power over me. I declare from this day forward, and this place of authority, that he will be blinded and will no longer disturb the straight ways of the Lord."

Have in mind what Paul did to that sorcerer Elymas, in the book of Acts 13:9-11 (NIV), "Then Saul, who was also called Paul, filled with the Holy Spirit, looked straight at Elymas and said, "You are a child of the devil and an enemy of everything that is right! You are full of all kinds of deceit and trickery. Will you never stop perverting the right ways of the Lord? Now the hand of the Lord is against you. You are going to be blind for a time, not even able to see the light of the sun." Immediately mist and darkness came over him, and he groped about, seeking someone to lead him by the hand."

This that I have told you is very powerful! You have the authority to break evil by the word of faith. Your life is hidden in Christ, with God (Colossians 3:3). We have to imitate Christ, our model. Author and finisher of our faith.

Look at Jesus Christ's reaction before Pontius Pilate, the Roman governor, ruler of the province of Galilee. This happened during his public trial. First, Pilate questioned Jesus, "Then Pilate said to Him, "Are You not speaking to me? Do You not know that I have power to crucify You and power to release You?" Jesus answered, "You could have no power at all against Me unless it had been given you from above" (John 19:10-11 NKJV).

In other words, Jesus was saying that what Pilate was doing to Him in that courtroom was only happening because it had been permitted in heaven—allowed by God for the salvation of humanity, previously pre-announced by His prophets.

Son/ daughter of God, listen: nobody can evict you from your job or destroy your business if you aren't allowed to in heaven. You cannot go bankrupt if in heaven you are prosperous. No one can curse you or bring you down if in heaven you are blessed. No one can bring you down to zero if in heaven your account is in abundance. There can be no curse against your sentimental and love life here on earth if you are blessed and graced in heaven. This is why you need to pray a lot, so that God's will be done on earth and in your life, according to the divine destiny and roadmap laid out in heaven for your life. Prayer helps to regularize your condition on earth, adjusting it in conformity with God's will. Heaven is our treasure; that is where our help comes from, from the Lord our God to deliver us and fight our battles. More are the angels who are with us than our enemies.

Keep this in mind; Satan can no longer go to heaven to do to us what he did to Job or Peter to sift him like wheat. This is one of the Good News for us: this thing of asking for access, the devil did it in the Old Testament, before Christ died on the cross for us. Now, we have an Advocate, to the Father, in the New Testament. In the Old Testament, Job didn't have an advocate.

God loved us so much and still loves us. For example, right now, in heaven, we have Jesus Christ, who is the Advocate and our High Priest. Furthermore, here on earth, we have the Holy Spirit, the "*Alos Paraclete*" - our Comforter (Counselor, Advocate, Intercessor, Helper, Substitute, Strengthener) (1 John 2:1; John 14:16).

Dear reader, we are made in life. And it is this awareness that you have to have every day.

Say it one more time out loud for the spirit world to hear, "I'm seated in the heavenly places, in Christ. What part of you is seated? Your spirit. So, with your body, you are working, sleeping, cooking, driving, among other activities: your spirit is placed in Christ, and your soul and body benefit from this glory. Because your body is the housing of the spirit that is saved, enlightened, and blessed.

With all boldness, you can now declare, "And raised me up together with him, and made me sit in the heavenly places in Christ Jesus."

In the three-dimensional plane, I'm alone, but in the fourth dimension, I'm in and with Christ. So I seem to be alone in the physical world, but in the spiritual world, I am not.

Starting today, every day, wake up early in the morning, and say to yourself, "I have been blessed with every spiritual blessing in the heavenly places in Christ Jesus. I'm seated in Christ above powers, above demons, above sorcerers, above every evil thing." Do this also before you go to bed to sleep.

Surrender to the Holy Spirit and don't look at the crises, attacks, or demons. Enjoy your salvation.

We can cancel the devil's plans because we are above the devil and his network. However, you cannot cancel the objectives of an entity above your ability. You can only do it for an entity over which you are superior.

For example, a father of a family can cancel the children's plans to leave home. But the children cannot stop their father from going home. This is because he has greater authority than they do, as long as they are under his roof.

Then, it's the one with the greater authority who can override the plans of the one with less authority. In this case, we have greater authority, and the devil has zero authority over us. After his resurrection from the dead, Jesus said, "All authority has been given to Me in heaven and on earth. Go therefore and make disciples of all the nations, baptizing them in the name of the Father and of the Son and of the Holy Spirit" (Matthew 28:18-19 NKJV). Jesus has given us this authority, all authority.

Listen to his words, "I have given you authority to trample on snakes and scorpions and to overcome all the power of the enemy; nothing will harm you" (Luke 10:19 NIV).

Activate your spiritual consciousness

Who are you? You are a son of God, a citizen of the Kingdom. You are seated in the heavenly places in Christ Jesus, the right hand of the majesty. You are ruling; you are reigning with Christ. He reigns on earth and fulfills his purposes through the Church.

Faith Confessions

Repeat these words:

- I'm reigning in Christ
- I'm reigning in health, spirit, and physical
- I'm reigning above the devil and his demons
- I'm reigning above all crises and circumstances
- I'm reigning, in the name of Jesus
- I know it's by God's grace
- I walk with dominion and live with prosperity
- I'm reigning

Every day, develop an intimate communion with Jesus. Know that your heavenly rule and your spiritual authority are nourished by the level of your surrender, your communion, your faithfulness, and your obedience to the LORD Jesus Christ.

Raise your hands now and thank God for what He has done for you and for where you are now. As you thank Him, pray for your family, your neighborhood, and your country. Cancel all the devil's plans, neutralize all evil. Pray with authority.

God bless you, richly

ABOUT THE AUTHOR

Onório Cutane

He is endowed with an apostolic-prophetic calling and serves as an apostle, teacher, and prophet. His divine mission is to propagate the gospel and deliver prophecies. Through his teaching ministry, as a devoted servant of God, he has brought healing and liberation to many, leading them from darkness into the realm of light and love. Onório Cutane is the esteemed founder and leader of Nations for Christ Ministerial Church. He is not only an author but also a songwriter and televangelist. His significant purpose is to advance the kingdom of Heaven and ready the Church for the second coming of Jesus. His ministry has a global reach, with congregations in Africa, Europe, Brazil, and the United States

DEDICATIONS

To the children of light and the intercessors spread all across the globe, who have been fighting spiritual battles daily against the forces of darkness for the sake of humanity; preserving it as the salt and illuminating it as the light of the world.

To humanity in general, for whom I have been praying and working during these ministerial years.

ACKNOWLEDGMENTS

To my beloved Lord Jesus Christ, for the grace he has given me to serve in his Kingdom and for the revelations in this book, his grace enables me.

To my dear wife and life companion, Janifer Cutane for always being by my side. To the Cutane Family for supporting me in this grand vision of reaching the nations of the world for Christ.

Other Books Also by Apostle Onório Cutane

1. **God's Medicine:** How to receive and maintain divine healing

2. **The Lordship of Jesus Christ and the Kingdom of Heaven:** how to live above the circumstances of this world

3. **Do not Break the wall:** Secrets to living under the divine protection

4. **The Good fight of faith:** how to fight and win. Secrets of constant victories in spiritual battles

5. **Grace to Reign:** secrets to living in God's grace and reigning in life

6. **The revelation of Jesus Christ:** who is Jesus Christ. Identity, Mission and mandate

7. **The four basic ministries of the believer.** Secrets to greatness in the kingdom of God

8. **The model father:** 11 Essential responsibilities of a father

9. **The four Essential habits of the new creation in Christ:** How to program your spirit for the glorious life;

10. **Prayer:** the believer's Spiritual Umbilical Cord. Concepts, Principles and Value

If you were blessed by this book and would like to share your testimony with us, you can send it to:

Email: books@ogcpublications.com

If you want to learn more about the Ministry and Messages in CDs or DVDs of Apostle Onório Cutane, you can access our website:

www.ogcpublications.com